PREPARING

DUMFRIES & GALLOWAY COLLEGE

Heathhall Dumfri

OWN CV

THE TIMES

PREPARING YOUR OWN CV

HOW TO IMPROVE YOUR CHANCES OF GETTING THE JOB YOU WANT

3RD EDITION

Rebecca Corfield

KOGAN PAGE

For YB

First published in 1990
Reprinted 1991, 1992, 1993, 1994, 1995 (twice), 1996, 1997 (twice)
Second edition 1999
Reprinted 2001
Third edition 2003

Kogan Page Limited
120 Pentonville Road
London N1 9JN
United Kingdom
www.kogan-page.co.uk

British Library Cataloguing in Publication Data

A CIP record for this book is available from the British Library.

ISBN 0 7494 3893 2

Typeset by Saxon Graphics Ltd, Derby
Printed and bound in Great Britain by Biddles Ltd, Guildford and King's Lynn
www.biddles.co.uk

Contents

Introduction

The world of work is changing fast. Many more of us will take temporary positions, have periods when we work on a freelance basis and move permanent jobs more frequently. Our careers are likely to change direction more than once in a lifetime of 40 years of working life. Job flexibility can mean job insecurity for some of us, forcing us to leave jobs before we want to, as employers' needs change and working roles are redefined. As a result, most of us will change careers and move in and out of different jobs many times in our working lives, perhaps going on training courses in between to make ourselves more employable.

This means that we are all applying for jobs more frequently in an increasingly competitive environment. Job-search skills that we used to need only at the start of a long period with one employer now need to be regularly honed and practised. The way that we present ourselves is crucial to being successful in today's job market. Every aspect of contact with a prospective employer needs to be as good as we can make it in order to impress.

Imagine this situation – you are looking to change your job when you notice an advert in the paper that seems right up your street. You are keen to put in an application until you realise that the advert specifies that you must send in your curriculum vitae – and you do not have one. What's more, you have never had such a document and are not sure exactly what it would look like.

The fact that you are reading this book is likely to mean that you are:

- looking for a job – perhaps you have been out of work for a while or have just finished a training scheme.
- trying to change your job – you may not be enjoying your current role or just feel that, for your career development, it is time to move on for some reason.
- planning a future change of career – whilst your job may be proceeding well at the moment, you may want to get ready for your next move in advance.
- preparing your personal job-search materials – even if there is no immediate prospect of a job change you may feel that it is sensible to keep your documents up to date just in case. You may want to check the current conventions and layout of CVs if you have not updated yours for some time.
- advising people in one of the above situations – you may be a careers or personal adviser, a teacher or a parent, wanting to keep your information about good practice current.

You know that the paper processes of applying for jobs are what make the difference in terms of attracting the right kind of attention from recruiters. The key to getting an interview rests on impressing an employer in writing in most cases. You have heard that a curriculum vitae or CV may help you get the job of your choice and need help to know where to start.

The importance of a good CV

Feeling that you are in the wrong career or that you cannot get the job of your choice can be very depressing. Finding a job, or a better job, is fraught with difficulties at the best of times.

Having to present yourself in a positive light when you are probably feeling overwhelmed, demoralised and not at your most self-confident may seem just too challenging. Even the most successful careerist can be anxious when it comes to applying for new jobs. In these circumstances you need the right help to compile a CV that will give you a big advantage in overcoming the hurdle of this lack of confidence that can affect any of us.

Anything that aids you in your job search is valuable but a good CV can be a real boon. A curriculum vitae is an extremely versatile document and it can enhance your job prospects regardless of your circumstances. You will benefit from compiling a curriculum vitae whether you have:

- many qualifications or none
- had many jobs, or never worked
- been unemployed for long periods
- experienced career success or have not yet found your niche
- excellent references or none.

When an employer is looking for an employee, one of the applicants has to be successful. That person could be you – as long as your CV stands out from the rest as being full of evidence that you are the best candidate for the job. Equally important, if this evidence is presented in a concise and attractive way, your CV can be a powerful influence working for you. In fact, your CV does not have to knock all the others off the employer's desk; it just has to be up there amongst the most impressive so that you get called in for an interview for the post.

Employers want an easy time when they are looking for suitable candidates to employ. If they can spot a good potential employee from the papers that arrive in response to an advert, they will spend much less time than usual in finding the right person for the job. Generally the numbers of people applying for every vacancy mean that any typically busy recruiters are looking for a way of reducing the number of CVs in front of them. Any that are less impressive, not as well presented or in some way disappointing, will be eagerly seized on – and thrown in the bin. This book shows you how to ensure that this does not happen to your CV.

However, there is an even more important reason for having your CV well prepared. Feeling in a position to apply for any job that takes your fancy or being ready to submit an application for a position that you hear of by chance, means that you are in control. It may sound like a small aspect of your life – it is after all one that is only represented by a couple of sheets of typed paper. However, if you think of the significance of being confident of your ability to represent yourself at any time, in a manner of which you can be proud, you can perhaps see how an impressive CV under your belt can just be the tip of the iceberg.

Sometimes life can knock us off course, events can be bewildering and being able to choose a career rather than just being able to find a job, any job, looks like an optimistic dream. Taking this small step to equip yourself with the best possible CV could be just the start of you gaining more confidence in your own ability to affect your future across the range of activities in your life. It is an assertive, self-confident, forward-looking act that could lead to lots of other changes in your life. Let us get started!

How to get the most out of this book

This book was written to guide you in your first steps towards putting together a curriculum vitae or CV for yourself – even if you have never heard the words before. Everything about the document will be explained for you. You do not need to be an expert at getting jobs, a high-flier or someone who is good at 'selling yourself' to other people. The curriculum vitae will do that for you.

Having the right CV is just part of the larger operation of finding a job – and that can be like playing a game. Several factors can help you to win in this game, and having a nicely written and presented CV is the place to start. Employers know roughly what type of person they are looking for, and you have to: (a) work out what they want; and then (b) convince them that you fit that description and are the candidate with the most to offer.

The advertisements below are typical of those seen every day. You will find job adverts in Jobcentres, employment agencies and newspapers, and on the Internet.

We offer a competitive salary, an enjoyable work environment, and benefits such as company discounts, concert tickets, and contributory pension scheme.

Please write with career details to

Margaret Smith
Recruitment & Training Officer
VP UK Limited
1 Oxford Street
London W1V 6HE

To apply for vacancies like these you need to have your own impressive CV ready to send off straight away. Once you have read through this book and used the practical advice to compile your own CV, you will have started to take more control over your role in job hunting, and the next steps will not seem so difficult.

Chapter 1 explains exactly what a CV is and shows what a standard layout looks like. In Chapter 2 we examine how to put the document to the best use. The most perfect of CVs is no good unless sent to the right places and targeted at the appropriate jobs. We study the content of a good CV in Chapter 3, detailing exactly what to include and what to leave out for the best effect. In Chapter 4 we look at how it should be physically presented for maximum impact.

PA-GROUP OFFICE
ADMINISTRATOR
based in PETERBOROUGH

We are the international headquarters for a new market-driven company, involved in the development and distribution of highly innovative home products.

The job: PA to our Chief Executive with UK and international responsibilities.

You are: Articulate and practical. You have excellent keyboard and other administrative abilities. You have good communication skills and can be part of a happy, ambitious team.

We offer: An excellent starting salary (£30,500, pension, medical insurance and generous performance bonus).

Please send your CV to: Mr Marcus Smith, Group Operations Manager, Aspen Lifestyle Products Ltd, Aspen House, Horsefair, Porterham PE1 5BQ.

In Chapter 5 you can look at a selection of real examples of other people's documents. This will enable you to learn from their best efforts before you start on your own CV. Different styles are illustrated and discussed here. Chapter 6 draws together all the information and gives you a step-by-step guide to compiling your own effective curriculum vitae. Chapter 7 indicates where you can find CV help on the Internet. You will find helpful dos and don'ts at the end of each chapter, and points to remember are highlighted as you work your way through the book.

What is a CV?

A CV is an outline, normally on paper, of a person's educational and professional history. This may sound as though it should only be used by 'professionals' or those with high-level qualifications, but *everyone* can benefit from having a well-written and well-presented CV when job hunting. It is a simple and accessible way of introducing yourself to potential employers and can be a vital tool in obtaining the chance to impress them face-to-face at an interview. Many employers and employment agencies will expect you to have your own CV ready and up to date. An increasing number of vacancies can be applied for by sending your CV online.

What does a CV look like?

Every CV will look different, and that is the way it should be. Like the real 'story of your life', it will be different from every other person's story, for each of us is unique. Written or typed on to paper, it is usually two to three pages long, printed on one side of the paper only. Black ink and white paper are most commonly used.

What does curriculum vitae mean?

The words come from the Latin (a 'dead' language now no longer used) and mean literally 'the course of your life' or the brief story of your career. The term is often abbreviated to CV, and these two letters are used to represent the term in this book. In some countries a CV is known as a résumé (pronounced 'rez-ume-ay').

Therefore, given the individual nature of this document, there is no such thing as the *right* way to construct a CV. Every careers adviser has different ideas about the best way to design and fill the document. Every employer will like to see this style or that layout. Each thinks that this or that should be included, in this or that manner. This book outlines the way I have found employers to be most impressed, and uses three simple rules that you will find repeated throughout the book:

1.   Keep it simple. An uncluttered document gets read before a fussy one. Plain layout of your document will help the reader to see how much you have to offer.
2.   Make it clear. Direct language and straightforward sentences are easy to read and understand.
3.   Keep it short. Less is often more when it comes to a CV.

In fact these rules should be applied to any written document, but are particularly important in a CV where only simple, clear and brief documents will be taken seriously.

What is in a CV?

Standard CVs are usually split into a maximum of seven different sections:

1.   *Personal details:*
      Includes name, address, telephone number, e-mail address, date of birth, nationality, etc. These are the facts about you and how to contact you.

2. *Education:*
   Provides dates, names and locations of schools and colleges attended and details of any qualifications that you may have obtained. This section also outlines the subjects that you have studied.

3. *Employment:*
   Specifies dates, employers' names and locations, job title and main activities/achievements of each position held. It is normal to begin with your current or most recent job.

4. *Other skills:*
   Covers your other practical abilities or skills, including training courses and other subjects studied, eg languages.

5. *Interests:*
   Includes hobbies, sport and leisure activities.

6. *Additional information:*
   Details other skills or type of work wanted. This section contains your statement about the contribution you can make and what kind of person you are.

7. *References:*
   Names, addresses and full contact details of two people who will provide character references for you.

How do you start to write a CV?

Welcome to the world of CV writing. If you have not approached this task before, you are about to discover the benefits of having such an aid to help you with your career development. Many people are worried about how to write this document. You may be someone who has been putting off writing your own CV, believing that it would be tricky or too demanding. You may even have not applied for vacancies if they asked for your CV because you did not know how to compile one. It is true that you will need to commit a certain amount of time and effort to the job, but you stand to gain a very valuable tool.

Writing a CV for yourself is time-consuming and laborious, but certainly worth the effort. The way to start is to read through this short book in order to understand the basics of compiling a CV. Then you can begin working through your own career history, guided by the examples contained in the book.

It would be much simpler if there were CVs in this book that you could just copy, but unfortunately, because each person has different experiences and skills, your CV *has* to be completely original, and unique to you alone. Although different CVs may look similar, each one will contain unique material.

Obviously, you can learn from other people and on pages 52–88 in Chapter 5 you will find many different examples of the way that CVs look once they have been put together. At the end of the book on pages 98–99, a blank form has been included for you to use when you start compiling a version for yourself.

The finished product will aim to:

- highlight the good points of your experience and skills. This means portraying what you have done and what you know in the best possible way.
- play down any weaknesses in your history. This means minimising any less successful times and covering up any gaps.

How long should a CV be?

Most CVs should be limited to just two sheets of A4 paper, so this document will not take you too long to write, once you know where to start and have help in presenting the information correctly.

When your CV is finished you will be able to update it regularly as you add to your experience and skills. The effort will be worth while and your confidence in presenting yourself to potential employers will grow when you see how impressive your history can look, once it has been well thought out and displayed.

Sometimes there may be justification for a slightly longer document but this only happens occasionally. Some examples could be:

- if you have had many different jobs and have worked for many years
- if you are in the entertainment business with many different appearances to list
- if you have travelled extensively with your work, eg with the armed services.

Points to remember

- Understanding the point of a CV will help you get inspired to get going.
- You will see many different styles of CV; you need to find one that you feel comfortable with.
- Stick to the simple headings recommended here in your CV, so that it appears uncluttered, rather than adding many more of your own.

Dos and don'ts

Dos

DO look at as many other people's CVs as you can for inspiration.

DO think about the kind of impression you want to convey to employers.

DO spend time thinking about the skills and qualities that are seen as valuable for the kind of position you are looking for.

Don'ts

DON'T reinvent the wheel – use good examples that you see in other CVs.

DON'T be too honest! We are aiming to minimise weaker areas and promote your good points.

DON'T hesitate! Get going on your first draft right now.

What is a CV used for?

A CV is a very flexible document and can be used for many different purposes. Here are just some examples of when a CV may be used:

- applying for advertised vacancies when the employer specifies that applicants must send in a CV – see the examples on pages 52–88. Employers want all applicants to submit similar documents in order to simplify sifting and short-listing. They will then be able to compare and contrast the strengths and attributes of the different candidates by checking through the CVs that arrive in the post.

- applying for vacancies in a speculative manner, or 'on spec'. This is when you write off to companies in the hope that they may have vacancies, now or in the future. If there are no current vacancies you can ask them to keep your name on file. Your CV can be a lasting record of your details for the company to refer to in case of employment opportunities in the future. You can find companies' names and addresses in newspapers, trade and telephone directories or on the Internet.

- by employment agencies or Jobcentres when they are putting your name forward to the employers on their books. An agency may gather a handful of the most appropriate

CVs to submit to an employer in the hope that one will be selected as right for the post.

- as an *aide-mémoire*, or memory-jogger, when you are completing application forms. All the information about your history will be included in this document, and this will save you from having to remember all the dates and information each time you have a different form to fill in.

- for general business purposes, when self-employed or doing consultancy work, etc. Your CV can act as a brief biography, outlining your experience and skills for any contract work that may require a bid from you.

- as an introduction to companies or banks when you need to explain your background for some purpose. CVs are not only of use when you are applying for work. Your finished document can serve as a summary of your background for other occasions.

- when making an application to a college for a course of study or training. Decisions about college places, particularly for mature candidates, may rest on how appropriate your background and experience have been for the subject to be studied. Your CV can help explain these aspects of your career to an admissions tutor.

How can a CV enhance your job prospects?

Have you ever seen a job that looked interesting, but have not applied for it because it asked you to send in your CV and you did not have one prepared? By the time the job is advertised, it is too late to draw up a CV from scratch so you can feel that you are unable to apply. This situation need never arise again.

Many jobs that are advertised in newspapers are filled very quickly indeed. If you can rush your CV to the company concerned, your application stands as good a chance as that of anyone else. However, if you are really keen on a job, it is no good dashing off a CV at the last minute. Hasty work will not match up to the best of the competition. An impressive CV needs time and care to compile.

Be prepared

Once you have produced a CV that you are pleased with, you have one big advantage over many other job-seekers: you are ready to apply for a job whenever a suitable one comes up. Instead of flying into a panic at the thought of having to prepare all your details, you will be ready to send off your personal introduction to the employer promptly.

Another great advantage of having an impressive CV to hand is that the same information can be sent to any number of different employers; the only information you need to change is the covering letter that is sent with it. Your CV will be deliberately designed to be suitable for many different situations.

How do you start to compile an effective CV?

Working on a CV that you are really proud of can take a long time. The finished document can be improved on and altered continually, even when you are ready to use it.

Making sure that you are including the right information is a time-consuming business initially. All your details need to be listed, and then you must be ruthless in weeding out any unnecessary information. A short CV is the only finished product that will be read.

Your CV will last your whole career long. It will change and develop as you do, but once written will provide the template that you can adapt as your experience grows and the requirements of the job market change. When the CV is looked at in this light, you can appreciate that it is going to be a very useful investment of your time, effort and writing ability to construct the best document you can.

You need to think of putting your CV together as though you were starting a major project at work or college. To do it properly you need to devote the necessary resources to it and take the task seriously:

- Get yourself mentally prepared. Enlist the help of family and friends by letting them know that you are embarking on this task and that it may take you some time.
- Treat it as work. This is not an activity to cram into odd minutes and spare moments. You will be preparing a well-written document that will last over the years, so take it seriously by ensuring that you have adequate time to devote to the task.
- Think about where and how you will do it. You need a quiet time and adequate space to:
  - sit and work
  - think and concentrate in a creative manner
  - collect source materials and deal with paperwork
  - write on a computer if you have one
  - use the telephone if you need to talk to other people
  - research different employers
  - print and edit documents
  - file documents and store finished copies.

The importance of presentation

Once you are happy with the content, the correct presentation of the document can be as challenging a task. A good CV will speak volumes about the sort of person you are. If you have taken the time to sort out the document properly, you will appear well organised and thorough (useful in any job), and if the CV is well presented, you will look as though you are a person who is careful about details and confident at the same time.

To start with, you will need to spend time collating the details of all the jobs you have done in the past, as well as the facts of your educational career. This may mean rooting around in old diaries or records and asking family members for their help. Certificates from school or college can provide useful education details and pay slips may tell you about the dates of jobs. Looking back through old photographs can sometimes help to jog your memory if you are stuck on exactly which dates are the correct ones. You may not want to include all this in the final version, but collecting everything together enables you to make clearer choices about what to keep in. One important point to bear in mind is that you want to be able to use the finished CV for more than one application, on more than one occasion.

A CV is never used on its own, and will always be accompanied by a covering letter (see the example at the end of Chapter 6 on page 95). This letter is your opportunity to be specific about exactly how you fit the particular job that you are applying for, picking out the relevant skills, qualifications or experience that you have detailed in your CV.

Stressing your good points

Writing the CV is excellent practice in being assertive about yourself and your achievements. Most people are hopelessly bad at putting their best points forward. We are all more used to being shy and quiet about our assets. But each of us is unique and has our own history, strengths and ambitions, and those that relate to you can shine out from your completed CV.

Job applications require you to be positive about everything you have been through so far, whether it be many different jobs, all for a short period, or bringing up children away from the paid work market.

This means that an added benefit of preparing your CV is that it helps to get you into the right state of mind to go all out for the job you want. It encourages you to think positively about what you have to offer and can act as your launching pad into the job market.

Minimising your weaknesses

Sometimes there will be aspects of your career history that you are not happy about. Although it would be wrong to be untruthful about your details, there are ways of accentuating those things which you *are* proud of, to take the attention away from anything else. This means that you maximise your achievements and minimise the rest. As we work through the different sections of the CV in the next chapter, looking at what information to include, we will consider ways of handling problem cases.

Even the most successful high-fliers will have some disappointments or embarrassments at some point in their career progress. The trick is not to emphasise these but to shine the spotlight instead on those aspects that enhance your potential and of which you are most proud.

Points to remember

- Turning the TV off and using quiet, soothing music may help you to get going.
- Thinking as widely as you can at the start will help you cover everything that you want to include.
- Working for hours can make you stale; keep having a break every 20 minutes or so to keep your concentration at its peak.
- If you get fed up and stuck, leave it alone, let some time elapse and then come back to it afresh.
- Getting others to look at what you have written can provide a valuable, different viewpoint.

Dos and don'ts

Dos

DO   get organised – it will help you prepare a better document in the long run.

DO   keep working on different drafts of your document until you are happy with it – this could mean three or four tries.

DO   keep positive. You need to feel upbeat in order to sell yourself in your CV.

Don'ts

DON'T   underestimate the time you will need, especially if this is your first attempt.

DON'T   start writing straight away – do some thinking and planning first about how you want it to look.

DON'T   get demoralised about the work involved. Think of all the people who have CVs; they will all have had to go through this process at some stage.

3

The content of your CV

What should be included?

So how do you start to put together your own CV? This chapter looks at *what* information to use, and Chapter 4 contains advice about *how* to present the information in the best way.

What you put into your CV is crucial to the way that it is perceived by the reader. This chapter outlines the main elements of a typical CV, and we will consider all the sections in turn in order to see what should and should not be included in each.

Remember the three important points mentioned in Chapter 1:

- Keep it simple.
- Make it clear.
- Keep it short.

Although there is no single right way to compile a CV, this is a tried and tested method of getting a good CV for yourself.

Even if you have never seen a CV before, you can use common sense to think about what a document like this needs to contain. For a start it must include identifying personal details as well as the facts about how and where you can be contacted. You will need to share your educational background and include your work history too. Describing your hobbies, interests and any other skills that you have can help to make your CV come alive. Referees' details will help any employer who may want to check you out in advance of meeting you.

If you are at the stage where you want to start compiling your own document, think broadly about what you could put into each section as it is described below. Make a note of anything that could be included. You can always cut the material back before you produce the finished version. This is much easier than having to add elements later.

Making your CV stand out

At the stage when your CV arrives on the employer's desk, he or she knows nothing more about you than the information that you are going to reveal in your CV. This means that you have a responsibility to do yourself justice, by explaining easily and simply who you are, and what you have done so far. You are an interesting and valuable person and your CV is the means by which you convey this to an employer.

The one way to ensure that your CV is noticed by an employer is to make it very obvious if you have done anything at all unusual. If you have travelled on a school or college trip, been involved with any voluntary groups or in different sporting activities, make sure you include these points.

You may be noticed by the employer just because there is something different about your CV which makes it stand out from all the others. If you can describe some activity that other people will not have taken part in, you will appear to have had different experiences from those of others, and therefore, to an employer, you may be more worth employing.

At this stage, all we are trying to do is to find out what material *could* be put into your CV. The amount of information that you compile may well end up being cut down a great deal, but that stage will come later on in this book.

Taking each section in turn, let us look at the CV for Patricia Mary Sharp, as an example:

1. Personal details

This section is usually not too difficult to compile, as it is just about the factual details of your life. Name, address and telephone number are put at the beginning of the CV so that your name and the way to contact you cannot be overlooked. Always include an e-mail address if you have one. This means that it would be easy for an interested employer to get in touch with you.

Name:
Names are written as:

Patricia SHARP.

Middle names are unnecessary as they will only confuse the reader, and how often do you ever use yours? The surname (or family name) should come at the end. This order of names makes more sense than Sharp Patricia, as this is not the way her name is normally used. We do not use P M Sharp either, as initials will also be difficult for an employer to understand and remember.

If you have more than one name (for instance married women who also use their maiden name), make sure you use the name that you would want to be called if you were employed as a result of the CV.

As some names can be unusual, it helps to put your second (or family name) in capital letters, so that it can be easily identified.

Address:
Always use your full address and postcode.

Telephone number:
Always include your telephone number if you have one. An interested employer may just want to pick up the phone in order to talk to you. If you are not on the telephone, try to find a friend or relative whose number you could use, so that messages could be taken on your behalf – as long as you are sure that they

will be taken reliably. Only use a work number if it really does not matter if you are called at work.

Put the full STD code and number, eg:

020 7928 0000 *or* Oxford (01865) 000000

to be as clear as possible.

Electronic mail:
Include your e-mail address if you have one. For many employers, it may be more convenient to contact you this way.

Date of birth:
15 July 1973 looks clearer than 15.07.73 or 15/7/73.

Use your date of birth rather than putting your age. If you write 37 this year, you will have to update it to 38 once your birthday arrives, and so on every year. If you feel that you are either particularly young or mature in age, do not be tempted to omit your date of birth. Employers are genuinely interested in your age, and there will be an opportunity under section 6, 'Additional Information', to add more details about yourself and to put your age in a positive light, should you feel it to be a disadvantage.

Nationality:
For some jobs, this aspect of your personal details is very important. If you are from another country, it is essential for you to specify that you are able to work here, eg:

Nigerian (with full UK work permit).

Refugee status is also worth mentioning, eg:

Ethiopian (with refugee status in the UK).

On the basis of keeping the information as simple as possible, some personal details which are not worth including are:

health, height, weight, place of birth, country of birth, unless you particularly wish to.

unless you have reason to think that including one of these factors in your CV would increase your chances of getting the job. For instance, if you were born in the place where the company is based, or if the job particularly requires a certain physical standard.

Some people include a recent head-and-shoulders photograph with their CV. I think that this can attract interest to your CV and get you noticed, particularly where physical appearance is relevant to the job, but the practice is still uncommon. For most positions, let the words do the talking and leave the picture out.

2. Education

This section is for you to outline your educational history from secondary school onwards. The further away this time is from the present, the less relevant the information will be. So, for instance, recent school leavers will give full details of all the subjects they studied in this section, as they will have less, or perhaps no information to put in the employment history section. More information on presenting a CV for a school leaver is included with the example on pages 52–54 in Chapter 5. If you left school and college many years ago and have been on more recent and relevant company or professional training courses, it may be worth while including them here. You may then want to call this section 'Education and Training' instead.

The information needed is, first, the dates that you attended your secondary school (from age 11 onwards) – either just the years, or the months and years. Next, the name and location of the school(s) should be included, although the whole address is not necessary. To locate a school, just the town and county or the city and postcode are appropriate. The last pieces of information are any examinations passed or, if none were taken, the subjects studied. You do not need to put down subjects in which you failed an exam – our intention is to stress strengths and minimise weaknesses. If you obtained distinctions, prizes or scholarships in certain subjects, include this information as it will set you apart from other candidates. If you worked on any particular projects, list these as well.

College details should be given in the same way. To use our example again, Patricia Sharp includes the following information:

1983–1988	Swansmead School Birmingham B14	**GCSEs:** English language Mathematics, History Science, CDT
1988–1990	Bishops Technical College Wolverhampton	**BTEC National Diploma:** Business Studies

As you can see from this example, school experience is usually put in chronological order, with your first school coming at the top of the list and then other periods of study listed in order, finishing with the most recent. College life offers more variety than the school experience in terms of courses or modules followed, learning opportunities and style of study undertaken. Give full details explaining what your college experience was like. If you were engaged in any extra-curricular activities such as clubs or societies that linked in with your studies, make a note of them here.

Typical problems

'My school career was a disappointment but I have studied and succeeded in my jobs since then. How can I make this late development look good?'

Retitle your Education section 'Education and Training' and list your professional courses there. Give full details of all the things you have learnt about. Use the 'Additional Information' section to talk about how you have gained a lot from your post-school studies, finding that training linked to work is especially rewarding and meaningful for you.

3. Employment

This section covers the different jobs that you have done. The information required is very similar to the last section on your educational details. You need to research all the starting and finishing dates of all the different jobs you have done, including part-time, vacation and voluntary jobs especially if you have not had much employment experience.

Either just the year, or the month and year, is again appropriate for each position. If you are older and have had many jobs, or have had gaps between jobs that you would like to 'smooth over', then just the year may be appropriate.

For this section, the order of your employment history is reversed. Starting with your most recent job, you list them all and end up with your first employment. The reason for this is so that the job in which you had the most responsibility, normally your last, comes first.

1987– 1990	Perkins Confectioners London SW15	**Clerical Assistant:** Word-processing, invoicing, dealing with customers, filing, telephone work, keeping petty cash.

The main difference between this section and the last is that here we need to say what the job title was in each case, and to specify the main duties for each different job.

You can see that only the main duties are listed, and they are written in note form. Also, they all begin with a verb: word-processing, invoicing, dealing with, filing, keeping, etc. To write full sentences would take up too much room. Although similar, this part of your CV is more difficult to complete than the last. You have to consider not only what to include but also how to describe the things that you have done in your work history. Most jobs involve many activities. You cannot list every single thing you did during years in one job but you need to do justice to the variety of key tasks that you undertook. These tasks represent what you learnt in the last job, and describing them enables you to demonstrate that you have these skills. It may well be that similar skills will be needed in the post for which you are now applying, and the employer needs to know that your experience is transferable to the new position.

Here is a list of words that could be useful to give you ideas about how to describe the work you have done in previous places of employment:

achieving
adapting
administering
advising
advocating
analysing
assessing
challenging
changing
checking
communicating
compiling
conducting
co-ordinating
creating
deciding
delegating
delivering
developing
diagnosing
discussing
enabling
establishing
evaluating
formulating

helping
initiating
inputting
leading
liaising
managing
modernising
monitoring
negotiating
organising
performing
persuading
planning
preparing
problem solving
producing
providing
recruiting
regulating
representing
researching
selecting
serving
supervising
training

Read through the list to see if the words apply to roles you have played in any of your previous jobs. There are many more active verbs than those used here but this list may inspire you to think of others that help to describe your work experience. Using positive and active words like these contributes to creating a powerful impression of a strong candidate. Your words on the page are all readers have to go on in terms of their perception of you. The more you can encourage their view to be of a dynamic and high-achieving writer, the better your chances of being invited to an interview.

Here are some more examples to show you how well these can come out.

1992– 1996	**Advertising Executive:** Responsible for running administration in the advertising section; liaising with advertising and PR companies, organising placing of adverts and promotions in different titles; developing office IT system for both Apple Macs and PCs; representing the company at the Frankfurt Book Fair.
1998– 2003	**Supervisor:** Managing group of seven; setting and monitoring budgets; planning production schedules and evaluating output; motivating staff and developing team working; achieved internal gold standard award for high performance together for three years running.
1993– 1997	**Manager/Partner:** Owner and manager of 50-seat floating restaurant, employing and supervising staff, setting up and monitoring systems, managing stock and sales, press and customer relations.
2001– 2003	**Administration Co-ordinator:** Organising car rental services across Europe, trouble-shooting, establishing and monitoring new client packages, dealing with European sales managers.

1999–	**Sales Assistant:**
2002	Serving customers; organising displays; dealing with problems; tidying stock; attending to health and safety matters; handling cash; participating in training and team meetings; developing my sales expertise.

If you have recently left school or college and do not have much or any work experience to put in this section, you need to think hard about what else you could use. If you have had any work experience, this is a useful substitute. Voluntary activities can be very helpful as they can provide the experience that employers are looking for. If you really have no experience at all of any kind of work, you need to fill that gap straight away. Contact your local volunteer bureau for opportunities for you to contribute to a local charity or voluntary organisation. There is something for everyone to do, and you will be able to find some way of helping that ties in with your interests. You may also be able to gain a job reference if you keep volunteering for some time.

Employers will be interested in the Employment section of your CV for the following reasons:

- to see if you have skills that are transferable to the job on offer;
- to check that you are able to work in a disciplined and structured environment;
- to look at the range and type of experience you have gained.

If the type of employment is not clear from the name of the company, and it is relevant to the job that you did, it is worth putting it in brackets after the name, eg:

Simpkins   **Clerk:**
(Solicitors)

Before you start to write up your own details, try to think of all the things that you did in each job, and list them all. Even though it may seem obvious to you that a clerical assistant would do some filing, it may not be clear to anyone who has not done exactly the same job before, and it may be just what the employer is looking for evidence of. Think through every-thing you did in each job, from the activities that occupied you when you started the job to those you were engaged in at the end.

The idea of a CV is that your history will be seen in date order. Remember, if you have had many large gaps in your employment history, you may find it more useful to put just the year of starting and finishing a job so that the end of each job merges more into the beginning of the next.

If you were in charge of other people in a job, make sure that you mention this at the beginning of your duties, and also include any promotions that you received during your time in the job. Were you involved with any special projects in any of your jobs? Did you sit on any working groups or take part in specific committees that added to your work role? Describe them in this part of your CV.

If you have had many different jobs, remember that the important fact is what sort of person you are now, and what skills and experience you have acquired to date. Jobs from further back may show your breadth of experience, but in that case they can be grouped together, such as:

'I have worked in many different types of employment during vacations, including shop, office and factory work'

or:

'I have four years of pay-roll and accounts work with agencies throughout the Birmingham area.'

I do not recommend including details either about why you left each job, or about what salary/wages you earned in each position. If the employer wishes to find out these things, they can be discussed in a subsequent interview.

4. Other skills

Include in this section any other skills that you have learnt that you would like an employer to know about. Examples could be familiarity with computer packages such as word processing or spreadsheets; first aid; full, clean driving licence; basic or advanced language ability.

Don't be tempted to undersell yourself here. If you can speak a language but not write it, then say 'Fluent in spoken Spanish' rather than 'Basic Spanish'. Most employers will be attracted more by spoken ability. Rack your brains to think of other practical skills that you have learnt over the years. Include any courses or training that you have undertaken that do not sit easily anywhere else.

5. Interests

Your interests can help to show that you have a well-rounded personality and do not live for work alone. Any interests that you have or have had in the past which are out of the ordinary will help you to stand out.

I would not recommend being too specific about any political or religious interests unless they are of direct relevance to the position that you are applying for. To make sure that you do not prejudice your chances, it is better to say that you are actively involved in the local community – the reader of your CV may hold different views from your own.

Try to put down some physical activities, as well as some cultural ones, to show that you are a healthy, active and lively person. Note form is all that is needed here, eg:

Swimming, karate, walking, travel, pottery, cinema and cookery.

You do not actually have to spend time on *all* these activities at the moment, but be sure that you know enough to talk about every interest you list at the interview. Employers often pick on your hobbies as an easy area of questioning. In this example, they may want to know what style of karate you studied. Not an easy question to answer if the nearest you ever got to karate was watching a Bruce Lee film, and the employer is a black belt!

If you belong to any clubs, societies or professional bodies, you can mention them here. Remember that an employer will be interested in any activity that makes yours stand out from the crowd of CVs that he or she is considering.

When making the decision about what information to include in this section, always remember that the point of putting down your hobbies is to show the reader that you are a well-rounded and balanced person, with a satisfactory life of your own outside work.

Try to avoid the most obvious interests, which we all share. This means that 'reading, socialising and watching TV' should be avoided.

6. Additional information or personal profile

With many CVs to consider, employers are looking for more than just the minimum skills and experience necessary to be able to do the job. They want people who will fit in the company or organisation properly. Therefore to get to the next stage of the recruitment process and be invited to an interview, your CV must also describe the sort of person you are. After all, you and I could have attended the same school or college and worked in the same places but we would still be completely different people.

To find material to use in this section, write a list of ten words or short phrases that describe your good points. The words in the list may be those that have been used about you in references or appraisals in the past, or compliments that have been paid to you when you have made a valuable contribution at work. They should describe some aspect of your personality rather than things you know how to do. The idea is to gather positive words that help portray your character at its best. Some words apply to just about all of us, so try not to include very obvious ones such as 'punctual', 'friendly' or 'sociable' in your ten.

Here is one list as an illustration:

- motivated;
- calm;
- polite;
- loyal;
- thorough;
- hardworking;
- serious-minded;
- accurate;
- determined;
- a good team worker.

Once you have compiled your list, pick the six or seven most relevant points to the kind of job you are likely to apply for. For each of the words or phrases, construct a sentence about yourself, where possible giving an example of when you have demonstrated that kind of behaviour and in this way work up a short passage about your personality.

From the list above, the result follows:

'I am a hardworking and loyal person. My experience working in shops has taught me that a polite and calm approach to caring for the customer works best. I try always to be accurate in my work and take a pride in being thorough about details. I enjoy working as part of a team.'

Here is the list of a completely different character:

- energetic;
- determined;
- keen to win;
- persuasive;
- ambitious;
- talkative;

- good sense of humour;
- creative;
- hardworking;
- quick learner.

The resulting paragraph from this list could be:

'My sales training built on my persuasive skills and natural determination. I learn quickly and my good sense of humour helps in any team when deadlines approach. I try to be creative in any task and work hard to contribute with energy and ambition to agreed team goals.'

Now compose your own list and paragraph. The result may sound as though you are blowing your own trumpet too much but please resist the temptation to include negative points or to qualify what you write as in 'fairly good', 'quite accurate' or 'usually hardworking'. Plain, positive words are needed here to allow your strengths to shine out of your CV. All other job applicants will be portraying themselves in the best light possible, so do not hold back. This section is normally written out in full sentences.

This section can be very important for those with gaps in the other sections of their CV. For instance, if you have brought up children and have therefore been out of paid work for some time, this is the place to explain the gap in your career. An example of this type of CV is included in Chapter 5, on pages 74–76.

If you have travelled for a time, you can write about it here. If you are changing career direction, this section is your chance to explain why you are interested in the new type of work.

Here are several examples of the type of information that could be included.

'For the last seven years I have been looking after my two children. This experience, coupled with my previous job, has taught me how to budget and plan, keep to deadlines, organise work schedules, work as part of a team and delegate tasks.'

'I am mature, very adaptable and can work cheerfully under pressure. I am painstaking in my work, honest, punctual and trustworthy. I make friends easily and enjoy working as part of a team.'

'I have many years' experience as a finisher in the clothing industry. After bringing up my family, I am eager to return to full-time employment and use my expert skills to contribute to an effective team. I can offer reliability, punctuality, stability and commitment.'

'During the past few years, I have spent a lot of time doing voluntary work in the community, both here and abroad, helping to provide for the needs of others.'

'I have extensive experience in designing, writing and testing programs, and versatile knowledge of software and operating systems.'

'I have a disciplined and organised approach towards my work, as well as being dependable, self-motivated and flexible. I am well presented and am an asset to any company I work for. My skills are highly transferable to any aspect of publishing.'

'I help to make things happen and am always reliable and enjoy moving projects forward. I am a confident, focused and well-motivated person. I combine an approachable appearance with the ability to empathise with others. I have strong convictions and am prepared to challenge when necessary. However, I take pride in being independent and objective in my consideration of issues, and entrepreneurial and innovative in my analysis.'

'I am a proficient organiser and experienced manager of projects and staff teams. Financial and resource management have been central requirements of my work. I maximise team efforts and motivation, which are critical to successful delivery, and in addition I provide leadership where necessary. I lead by example, enabling others to develop confidence in their own abilities.'

'Following three O levels, I achieved academic success after 20 years outside education with an MA in Marketing, linking communicating with campaigning. I see myself as a change agent, modernising and adapting structures, and assessing and helping to deliver changes. I was able to concentrate on succession planning, spotting potential stars on the staff, developing, nurturing and fast-tracking future Regional Officers.'

'I combine management experience at the sharp end of training with an understanding of the private sector and a readiness to take on the responsibility for organisational strategy at all levels. The centre I run began in 2000 as a good idea that needed fostering and developing. I have provided a clear vision of its future and effective team direction, and today it is a flourishing success story. My enthusiasm, calm approach to problem solving and commitment to the highest professional standards ensure quality of provision for clients and value for money for project partners.'

This additional information part of your CV is sometimes called a 'personal profile'. There are different ways of approaching the layout of this section and these will be covered in the next two chapters when we look at how to present your CV.

7. References

You should name here two people who can be approached to provide a reference for you. One should be your last employer or someone from your last school or college, and the other should be a friend. The reference from your last employer can just be given as the Personnel Department of a large firm, if there is no particular person to write it for you.

The reason for references is so that the reader can see that you have referees who are prepared to vouch for your competence and character. They will often be contacted, so you must make sure that you ask their permission first.

If you are sending your CV out to many addresses, make sure that your referees are happy about being contacted by a variety of people over a long period. You cannot afford to have an employer contact someone whose name you have given as a referee, only to be told that he or she does not want to vouch for you.

Character referees should normally have a good job of their own, and must not be in your own family, although if a family member has a different name from yours (such as an in-law), nobody would know that you were related. Family doctors or priests can often be prevailed upon to act as referees if they have known you for some time, but again you must get their permission first.

Include a telephone number for both references if possible, as the employer may well just decide to pick up the telephone on the spur of the moment. Before you give out home telephone numbers, check that this is acceptable to your referees. If you are applying for various vacancies it can be helpful to discuss the nature of each particular job with your referees to help them target the information they provide to the prospective employer. Many e-mail requests are made for references these days, so including e-mail addresses can be helpful.

Please remember that anyone who is prepared to write a reference for you is doing you a big favour. Regular appreciation makes sure all your referees feel properly valued by you.

If you have recently arrived in this country or have been travelling, and only have references from another country, I strongly advise you to contact the referees and get them to write an open letter or testimonial on your behalf. This can be used each time you send off your CV: send a photocopy (never send the original) of the letter, attached to the back of your CV.

The reason for this is that many employers are put off by the fact that it will take them a number of weeks to get a reference for you, but if they can see the testimonial in front of them, it may not prejudice them against you. In this case, only your two references are needed. Do not be tempted to include lots of photocopies of testimonials or exam certificates, as great wodges of paper will just put the employer off.

Typical problems

'I was sacked from my last job, and I know they will give me a bad reference.'

This can be overcome by using an earlier employer for the reference, and explaining why in an interview. You can say that you experienced personal difficulties in your last employment. You will have to rehearse your description of the events exactly, before any interview, to make sure that you can sound convincing.

If you have only had one job and been sacked, you will have to try and put the situation in the best light possible to explain what happened. Use two personal references on your CV. Perhaps you could do some voluntary work to give yourself another reference – even if only for a short time.

'I can get an excellent reference from my last employer, but she spends long periods out of the country. Should I still include her as one of my referees?'

Anything that is likely to put a prospective employer off is a bad idea. If the employer is interested in taking you on, he or she will not want to wait for six months before receiving your reference. I would advise you to find a substitute referee who can guarantee a quick response to any enquiries. Another alternative is to get an open testimonial from this woman explaining that she is often unavailable, which you could then include with your CV.

Points to remember

- Think widely about what you have done and include everything in your first draft.
- You can always trim your CV later but enlarging it may mean you have to start again from scratch.
- Be positive when you describe your past activities; this can only impress any reader.

Dos and don'ts

Dos

DO   get in an upbeat mood before you start work on this draft of your CV; it can make a big difference to your output.

DO   enhance your creative thinking by getting your environment as congenial as possible when you are working on the document.

DO   talk to people who have known you in different roles; they may come up with tasks, activities and achievements that you had forgotten.

Don'ts

DON'T   get bogged down in your own history. If the detail of one job escapes you, move on and think about another until your memory returns more clearly.

DON'T   make things up. You need to be truthful about the work experience you have had. Even if what you write fools the employer, liars tend to get found out at the interview stage.

DON'T   downplay your skills and experience by writing weak descriptions. Show off all the talents you have – every other candidate will do so too.

4

Presentation

After your work on collating material for the content of your CV, you are ready to consider how to present the document. The decisions you make about layout and presentation are as significant as the content you include.

You can now collect together all the material that you need to put into your CV. The way that you present the CV is of the utmost importance. You know that when you buy goods, you are often attracted by the packaging on the outside as much as by what is inside. The same is true of the CV. Giving employers your notes to read would leave them scratching their heads in confusion about what it all means, and they would probably not be very impressed.

After all, that is the whole point of compiling a CV in the first place. You want to present yourself in the best possible light to employers, and the way that they will judge you is by the impression they gain from those two sheets of A4 paper. For that is the only information they have to go on. Everything in this chapter is to further that aim.

When thinking about presenting your CV in the best way try to avoid anything that might put an employer off. This means that the CV must look:

- plain. An unadorned document says that you are businesslike and purposeful. Too many decorations, font variations and design complexities detract from an overall positive impression.

- attractive. Choose a sans serif font or typeface for your document for an unfussy, compact style. Good fonts to use include Arial or Helvetica.
- easy to read. Without wasting paper unnecessarily, you should allow generous margins and reasonable space between columns. Allow a clear line space after each paragraph.

Written, typed or word-processed?

If at all possible, get your CV done on a computer, even if you have to pay for the privilege. It will come out typed, can be edited without difficulty, and has the great advantage of being easily updated at any time in the future.

Do not attempt to word-process your own document if you have never used a computer before and cannot type. It will take you ages and you will probably make many mistakes as well. You can pay to have your CV typed by somebody else, but shop around before you pay out a lot of money, to make sure that you get the best deal possible.

These days, many people have computers at home, and you may be able to find a friend who will help you to get it done. The great advantages of computers are that you can make any corrections easily and you can run off as many copies as you like, whenever you want them.

The second best alternative is to have your CV typed. It looks smart and professional but will have to be completely re-typed if any of your details change. Never be tempted to use correction fluid to make changes to your CV, or to add information using a different machine, as it will look messy.

If it is at all possible, have your CV word-processed or typed up. Your local Jobcentre may be able to find a place to get this done if you are not working and need help with this task.

Order

The order of the different sections recommended in the last chapter has been tried and tested many times. The simplicity of the design seems to impress and interest employers.

The beauty of this standard layout is that the contents follow a logical pattern. First you are introducing yourself, then saying where you have come from, in terms of your education and employment experience. You then go on to explain your other skills and any other relevant information, including your interests and referees. You are telling the complete story.

Other styles

US style

An alternative way to order your material on the page is to have the additional information about your personality and achievements (sometimes called a 'personal profile') at the start of the document. This arrangement of contents means that the first thing that the reader sees is the paragraph explaining the special features about you. This is a more obviously direct and punchy way to start the CV and tends to be the dominant style in US CVs (or résumés). It allows readers to decide up front if they like the sound of the candidate or not. The slight drawback of this more forthright style is that the reader may just decide not to continue reading. With the additional information at the end of the CV, the reader is drawn or led through the whole document, and the personality of the writer is only revealed at the end. An example of the US style is shown on pages 83–85.

Freestyle

CVs can be written in any style you like, with the information displayed in a variety of different layouts. That is the beauty of the document – you can select the order of the material that you feel will best reflect the contribution you can make to the job in question. If you feel that the employer will be more interested in a description of your relevant skills, you could choose to have these as subheadings through the document and then just summarise your educational and employment history elsewhere. See the example on pages 86–88 to illustrate this kind of tailored layout of a CV. If you feel that your work experience needs enlivening, you could add a separate subheading for 'Achievements' either under each position held or after the details of your jobs.

Length

Your CV should not take up more than two sheets of A4 paper using one side only. Some people have difficulty in stretching their CVs past one side, particularly if they have little experience of work. Often a CV will stretch over four or five sides of A4 at the first draft. Let us look at each of these problems in turn.

Typical problems
'My CV is too short.'

If you have just left school it will be necessary to make your CV more of a personal information sheet. This gives you much more scope for including information about other activities that you have taken part in at school or college. For instance, you can describe your role in teams that you have played in or groups that you joined. See the example on page 53 of Chapter 5.

If you took GCSEs at school you should be able to include your record of achievement, which charts your progress through the fourth and fifth years. You may wish to have one sheet of personal information with your record of achievement attached, or you could use the record to give you more details for your CV.

'My CV is too long.'

You must reduce the length of your CV to two sides if possible. Nobody reads more than two sides. Imagine you are a busy personnel officer desperately trying to check through the pile of CVs on your desk. With 20 to read in half an hour, you would find any excuse to reduce the pile by one.

The exceptions to this rule are older graduates who may have many college courses and jobs to fit in or those who have had many different jobs over a long time period. On no account should *any* CV be longer than three sides of A4 paper.

'My CV covers more than one side of A4, but only reaches half way down the second.'

Stretch the whole document out (easy on a computer) until it covers the two sides easily. In other words, add more space around your name, to help it stand out, and make bigger gaps between the different sections. Place the referees one beneath the other instead of next to each other. The more white space showing on the CV, the easier it will be to read.

'I now have six pages of rough draft for my CV. How will it all fit on to two sides of A4?'

Be ruthless! Remember – keep it simple, make it clear, keep it short. Use brief phrases, in note form, for the details of your education and employment experience. Edit your work to the bone, even if that means drafting the CV four or five times more. Make it look crisp and concise in the final version. If in doubt, throw it out!

Layout

Dense, tightly packed typing is very difficult to read. Therefore spread out your words evenly and neatly on the page to aid the reader.

Use white or very light paper as it will often be photocopied once at the employer's premises and dark colours do not copy well. However, a heavier weight of paper is worth using as it can make your CV stand out from the rest. Buy a box of 100 gram weight paper, perhaps with friends to share the cost. Be careful to check though that the paper you buy will run through the printer you use. Some heavier paper creases and jams in certain more sensitive or older printers.

Keep it simple

I have seen a badly laid out CV in which the author had experimented with many different typefaces or types of print. The result was a complete mishmash of styles and shapes. It put off anyone reading such a confusing document.

Never use more than two different fonts on your CV. More does not mean better-looking. Use different sizes of the same typeface if you want to add some definition for side headings but do not let them dominate the eye at the expense of the important details about you: your name, qualifications and job titles.

Adding emphasis

There are certain features about your CV that you will want to jump out at the reader. The main one is your name. If the employer is sifting through a pile of 20 CVs, you must make sure that yours is easy to spot and remember. If you can use a word processor, put your name in bold or in a slightly larger size font. If the document is typed, underline or double-type it.

Other things to be put in bold, underlined or in some way highlighted are the level of exams you have taken (GCSEs, A levels, etc) and the position of each job that you have held (kitchen porter, journalist, marketing manager, etc). Do not be tempted to highlight the fact that the title of this document is Curriculum Vitae. If the reader cannot tell what the document is, he or she will not be giving it enough attention to act on it anyway. You also do not need to highlight the subheadings such as 'Name', 'Address', etc through to 'References' either. Your details are what we want to call attention to, and the way to do that is to highlight your achievements in terms of your exams, or courses studied and your job titles.

Look at the examples of CVs in the next chapter to see how impressive this suggested layout looks.

A more creative or varied layout of your CV may possibly be appropriate if you work in a very design-conscious field, but generally I would advise caution. It is better to have a plainer document that is easy to read than a jazzy one that might put people off if they do not share your taste in graphics.

Sending your CV by e-mail

Rather than printing off your CV and posting it in application for a vacancy, you may want to use electronic mail or e-mail to send it to the employer. This could be because:

- You are sending the CV to an employer's or recruitment agency's Web site.
- You are circulating your CV to a range of employers on a speculative basis via the Internet.
- The employer has specified in an advertisement that you should e-mail the CV.
- You are choosing e-mail because it suits your own administration better.
- You need to get the document there instantly.

Unless you have been specifically asked to e-mail the CV, if you are applying for a specific vacancy it is worth also sending a printed-out version on paper (also known as a 'hard copy') in the post afterwards. This is the form of the document that is preferred for photocopying and distributing by most employers and saves them the trouble of printing off the document themselves. It also ensures that you have sent a good-looking copy for them to see. Your beautiful e-mailed version may print out sadly askew on a different brand, style or age of printer.

If you are to e-mail the document it is even more important that you use simple fonts or typeface when putting it together on your computer. Arial and Helvetica are modern-looking, simply styled fonts that you can be more confident will print out properly at the employer's end. Make sure you write and save your CV in the Microsoft Word word-processing package as it otherwise may emerge with disturbed layouts or even as total gobbledegook if the employer's computer facilities do not match your own. Pages of incomprehensible rubbish spewing from the printer will not enhance the impression you are making!

Points to remember

- The look of your CV is at least as significant as what is in it.
- You are in charge of choosing the best way of presenting the document.
- A simple, uncluttered style says that you are a focused and professional applicant.
- Unless you send a hard copy in the post, you cannot be sure how your CV looks to the employer.

Dos and don'ts

Dos

DO   show your CV to different people and ask for their opinion of the layout.

DO   check spelling and grammar if you are in any doubt about anything.

DO   spread the content evenly through the available space; it is kinder on the eye and encourages the reader to continue.

Don'ts

DON'T   leave anything in that you don't think adds to the total effect.

DON'T   worry if the laying out of the CV is a fiddly business. It normally takes as long as finding the content did.

DON'T   photocopy your CV if it is possible to print off fresh copies each time.

5

Guidelines and examples

Dos and don'ts

From the information that has been covered so far, there are some general, basic rules to follow when making a good CV for yourself.

Dos

DO   keep it simple – avoid putting the reader off with long words or sentences.

DO   make it clear – all the information should be easy to understand.

DO   keep it short – two pages maximum if possible. If in doubt, throw it out.

DO   be positive – do not elaborate on jobs that you did not make a great success of, or finish; accent instead what you *did* achieve in the situation. For instance, even if you did not gain any exam passes at school or college, still list the subjects that you studied.

DO   assume that the reader does not know what you did in your different jobs; the thing that you think is obvious may not be so to the reader.

DO   take time to put your CV together, and be prepared to make lots of rough notes about your career history first. Chapter 6 takes you through a step-by-step guide to getting started.

DO   experiment to see the effect of different aspects of your skills and achievements being highlighted.

DO   have two (or more) different versions of your CV if you need to apply for jobs in different career areas – but make sure to note which CV you send off to each employer.

DO   get to know your CV inside out – to enable you to talk positively about yourself in an interview.

DO   get the finished product word-processed if at all possible.

DO   update your CV whenever you have new experiences, qualifications or additional information to include.

Don'ts

DON'T   use jargon, or you risk confusing and losing the reader.

DON'T   use pretentious language; write as you would speak – simply and clearly.

DON'T   copy someone else's CV – it will always look fake.

DON'T   invent information – you may well have to prove your knowledge in an interview.

DON'T   lie about yourself. You can be dismissed from a job if such misrepresentations are discovered.

DON'T   worry about boasting about your strengths – everybody else will be making themselves look extra good too.

DON'T   send out the original of your CV if it is difficult for
         you to get copies. Good photocopies should be used
         for sending to employers and the original kept clean
         and safe.

DON'T   run out of copies to send out – that will be the time
         when the job you *really* want comes up.

Examples of CVs

The following pages contain 12 examples of CVs for people in
different situations. One or more of them may be relevant to
you, as you are thinking about what to put in your own CV.

These examples are only included to give you an idea of the
many different ways that CVs can be written. Although the
names and addresses are fictitious, all the details have been
taken from real examples of CVs that have helped people to get
the jobs they want. See if you can identify how they use the
points made earlier in this book about content and style.

There is not a CV for every situation, but the examples have
been specially picked to represent a wide range of types of CV.
Do not copy the information included in the examples, but see
if any of them would be an appropriate model for you on which
to base your own information.

These are the CVs that are included:

1. School leaver
2. College leaver
3. Graduate (Version 1)
4. Graduate (Version 2)
5. Voluntary experience
6. Many jobs
7. Gaps between jobs
8. Woman returner
9. Career changer
10. Made redundant
11. US style
12. Freestyle.

1. School leaver

CURRICULUM VITAE

NAME: **Moira MAGUIRE**

ADDRESS: 18 Horton Gardens
                      Nunhead Road
                      London SE16 1QJ

TELEPHONE: 020 7338 0000

DATE OF BIRTH: 18 August 1986

NATIONALITY: British

EDUCATION:

| Sept 1997– | Stone School | **Subjects studied:** |
| July 2002 | London SE16 | English, mathematics, science, history, drama |

GCSEs:

English	C
Mathematics	C
Science	D

EMPLOYMENT:

| June 2000 | Azir's Newsagent | **Sunday papergirl:** |
| to date | London SE16 | sorting out and delivering papers and handling cash |

VOLUNTARY WORK:
Since my final year at school I have worked with the elderly
housebound. I regularly visit three people who live locally and
help them with shopping and other household tasks. I find this
work stimulating and rewarding, and intend to continue with it
in my spare time.

OTHER SKILLS:
I was the House Captain in my last year at school and helped to
organise assemblies and sports days. I can type at 45 wpm and
am confident at using a word processor. I plan to learn to drive
next year.

INTERESTS:
Martial arts, bronze medal for swimming, skateboarding,
cookery and embroidery.

ADDITIONAL INFORMATION:
I am a polite and co-operative person and I apply myself totally
to the task in hand. I am a member of my local youth group and
regularly attend the swimming club. Since the third year I have
been in the school drama group and have appeared in many
productions.

REFERENCES:
Mr Azir (Proprietor)
Azir's Newsagent
218 Watermill Road
London SE16 1HC

Tel: 020 7990 0000

Ms Hardcastle, Head Teacher
Stone School
Lovelace Road
London SE16 3PP

Tel: 020 7731 0000

Moira has no full-time work experience yet, but has managed to get herself a part-time job delivering newspapers. This now provides evidence that she is capable of sticking to a work routine, is trustworthy and determined.

Even without this, she can write about her voluntary experience working with old people while still at school. This implies that she has the ability to get on with a variety of different people, and shows her patience and her concern for others.

Her CV looks very different from most of the others on the following pages because she does not have a list of different jobs that she has done. However, although she has less information than many others, the fact that she has prepared a CV for herself will impress potential employers by setting her apart from other young people of her age.

She has included some interests which make her stand out from other school leavers – martial arts and skateboarding – which also give her topics to discuss at an interview.

Her CV is not much more than her personal details – in fact it could be called a 'Personal Information Sheet' rather than a CV – but it still tells the story of her career to date.

If you know that your own CV falls short in some area, eg little work experience or not many examination passes from school, then you need to find a way of compensating for this. You will need to show more evidence in different areas that make up for the gap. Moira does this by showing alternative work experience (part-time and voluntary) to make up for the fact that she has only just left school. Missing out on some area of experience or qualifications need not be an insurmountable hurdle to impressing an employer. You just need to show that what you lack in one area you more than make up for in another.

2. College leaver

CURRICULUM VITAE

NAME: **Robin FOSTER**

ADDRESS: 222 Upper Street
                    London N1 5DJ

TELEPHONE: 020 7278 0000

DATE OF BIRTH: 18 June 1982

NATIONALITY: British

MARITAL STATUS: Single

EDUCATION:

1993– 1998	Kingsmere Secondary School London E5	**GCSEs:** English C, Maths B, Physics B, Chemistry C, Geography B, Biology B, Sociology B, French E
1998– 2000	South West London College London SW15	**A levels:** Maths A, Biology C Physics E
2000– 2003	Peele University Peele Northants	**BA Social Science:** Studied economics, history, politics, philosophy, geography and statistics **Specialised in:** Development studies. My thesis was on Third World debt

EMPLOYMENT:

Both my jobs have been part time, and took place during vacations and evenings while at college.

| 2001 | Peele University Union | **Bar Attendant** |
| 2002 | Peele University Catering | **Catering Assistant** |

OTHER SKILLS:

I can use a computer and am familiar with several word-processing and spreadsheet packages.

INTERESTS:

Keep fit (I was a member of several sports societies while at college), reading, travel, music.

ADDITIONAL INFORMATION:

Having successfully completed my course at Peele University, I am looking to gain employment in an administrative capacity, general office work, or work involving figures. I always contribute fully and would enjoy maintaining high standards of accuracy and attention to detail. I am keen to start my career and would be a loyal and dependable employee.

REFERENCES:

Professor S Welt
Peele University
Peele
Northants NT5 5BG

Tel: 01772 00000

Dr L M Cash
97 The Crescent
London W5 2PB

Tel: 020 8435 0000

Robin has made the most of the space available to him to give full information about his college career. He has given detailed information about his course at college and about the jobs he did while studying. Without any full-time work experience, he needs to bring out any other factors which may help to persuade a future employer that he is worth taking on.

He mentions his active involvement in sport to show that he has a variety of interests. He also uses the 'Additional Information' section as a chance to sell himself to the employer. He stresses his good points to show the contribution he could make.

He knows that he has to use his CV to enable the employer to envisage him at work. His main selling point is the potential contribution he could make if employed. Robin makes clear in the 'Additional Information' section that administrative work and figure work are areas where he thinks he could make the strongest application. He could well be sending this CV off on a speculative basis in case vacancies arise at a specific company or organisation.

3. Graduate (Version 1)

CURRICULUM VITAE

NAME: **Michael SMITH**

ADDRESS: 935 Main Road
                       Manchester M16 8AP

TELEPHONE: 0161-693 0000

DATE OF BIRTH: 27 August 1978

MARITAL STATUS: Married

EDUCATION:

1989– 1996	Frankwell Secondary School Shrewsbury Shropshire	**GCSEs:** Seven subjects including English Language, Literature and Mathematics **A levels:** Mathematics B, Geography C
1996– 1999	Lowston Polytechnic Lowston Surrey	**BA (Hons) Business Studies:** Specialised in marketing and financial management
2002– 2003	London Massage School London SW18	**ITEC Course in Massage, Anatomy and Physiology:** Training in techniques to give professional, therapeutic treatment, allied with a sound knowledge of the systems of the body and their relevance to massage
2003– date	London Massage School London SW18	**Intermediate Massage Training Course:** Continued training by studying shiatsu, medical massage, reflexology and breathing and relaxation techniques

EMPLOYMENT:

2001–	Private work	**Consultant Masseur:**
2003	in the London area	Relaxing, professional therapeutic massage with essential oils

1999–	Employment agencies	**Various clerical positions:**
2001	in the London area	General office work and dealing with the public

OTHER SKILLS:
I have a working knowledge of aromatherapy, reflexology and shiatsu. I have a current, clean driving licence and have recently acquired basic keyboard skills.

ADDITIONAL INFORMATION:
I have always used my hands in a creative way, and found massage a natural progression, which is immensely rewarding and fulfilling.

I am a friendly, outgoing person, and am able to get on with people in all situations. I am reliable, trustworthy, punctual and meticulous. I have the ability to work well as part of a team, can deal competently with administrative duties and particularly enjoyed the financial aspects of my business course.

REFEREES:
Bernadette Beckett (Principal)
London Massage School
Westcliffe Road
London SW18 2HB

Tel: 020 8339 0000

Clare Maledy (Course Tutor)
BA Business Studies
Lowston Polytechnic
Lee Street
Lowston
Surrey KT3 2MN

Tel: 020 8448 0000

Michael is trying to use his massage qualification to get a job in a health or sports centre. However, his background is in business studies, so he uses the 'Additional Information' section of his CV to explain his interest in massage.

He gives most details about his interest in massage, the subjects that he studied in his practical training and the fact that he has spent a period self-employed as a masseur.

He is still considering a career in business, so he has created another CV, to apply for a different type of work.

Sometimes you can have more than one career in mind. You may have talents that lie in different directions or just want to keep your options open if you are just starting your working life. In this case you may well need more than one CV to reflect adequately your different career possibilities. With two documents you can stress separate aspects of your skills and abilities to tailor your CV for the particular career in question.

4. Graduate (Version 2)

CURRICULUM VITAE

NAME: **Michael SMITH**

ADDRESS: 935 Main Road
                         Manchester M16 8AP

TELEPHONE: 0161-693 0000

DATE OF BIRTH: 27 August 1978

MARITAL STATUS: Married

EDUCATION:

1989–1996	Frankwell Secondary School Shrewsbury Shropshire	**GCSEs:** Seven subjects including English Language, Literature and Mathematics
		A levels: Mathematics B, Geography C
1996–1999	Lowston Polytechnic Lowston Surrey	**BA (Hons) Business Studies:** Specialised in marketing and financial management, completed thesis on European business training
2002–2003	London Massage School London SW18	**ITEC Course in Massage, Anatomy and Physiology:** Training in techniques to give all types of massage, currently studying at intermediate level

EMPLOYMENT:

2001– 2003	Self-employed in the London area	**Consultant Masseur:** Relaxing, professional therapeutic massage with essential oils
1999– 2001	Employment agencies in the London area	**Various clerical positions:** Dealing with the public and filing, answering phone calls, writing letters, typing, keeping petty cash account

OTHER SKILLS:

I am a keen masseur, and have a working knowledge of aromatherapy, reflexology and shiatsu. I have a current, clean driving licence and have recently acquired basic keyboard skills.

ADDITIONAL INFORMATION:

I enjoyed my degree course which introduced me to the business world. I specialised in financial analysis and the marketing function, and completed my thesis on the different types of business trading across Europe.

I am a friendly, outgoing person, and am able to get on with people in all situations. I am reliable, trustworthy, punctual and meticulous. I have the ability to work well as part of a team, can deal competently with administrative duties and am keen to establish my career in a clerical or administrative capacity.

REFEREES:

Clare Maledy (Course Tutor)
BA Business Studies
Lowston Polytechnic
Lee Street
Lowston
Surrey KT3 2MN

Tel: 020 8448 0000

Bernadette Beckett (Principal)
London Massage School
Westcliffe Road
London SW18 2HB

Tel: 020 8339 0000

It would be difficult for Michael to have just one CV which detailed all the information that he needs to apply for both the types of work that he is interested in.

His second CV has the same basic information about his personal details, qualifications and experience, but stresses his interest in a career in administration instead of massage. He includes more information about his college course, his office experience and changes the 'Additional Information' section to appeal more to employers of clerical staff.

These two CVs, sent out with care to appropriate employers, will enhance his chances of gaining one of the types of employment of his choice.

This example shows that Michael has created two impressive documents to reflect his job hunting. If he had relied on just one CV, he would have found it difficult to straddle both options whilst making the CV interesting. By creating the second, more business-oriented CV he can keep the focus of each targeted at the kind of employers he would like to work for, highlight the respective skills and aptitudes he has and show the full contribution that he could make in each case.

5. Voluntary experience

CURRICULUM VITAE

NAME:	**Geraldine CLARKE**
ADDRESS:	99 Eugenia House Norton Street Chipping Campden Gloucestershire GL2 1KK
TELEPHONE:	016732 0000
DATE OF BIRTH:	14 April 1976
NATIONALITY:	British

EDUCATION:

1987– 1992	Josiah Wedgwood School London NE21	**GCSEs:** English, Maths, French, Technical Drawing and Art
1992– 1996	North London Technical College London NE17	**BTEC National Diploma:** Visual research, objective drawing, furniture design, drawing office practice, foundation science, industrial organisation
		BTEC Higher National Diploma: Antique history and restoration specialising in gilding and Victoriana

VOLUNTARY EXPERIENCE:

1996– 2002	Green World Bath Avon	**Membership Secretary:** Dealing with all letter and phone enquiries, setting up new computer system and helping to train paid staff

HOBBIES AND INTERESTS:

I enjoy photography, reading, windsurfing, sailing, skiing and going to the cinema and theatre.

ADDITIONAL INFORMATION:

Since leaving college, I have been looking after a sick relative. I used my two free days each week to volunteer for a local charity. During the last six years I have become very involved in their business, and have recently been part of a team which designed and established a new computerised membership system.

Although this work was unpaid, the skills I have gained are those used in any business environment, such as being part of a team, keeping to deadlines, working under pressure and delegating tasks.

I enjoyed learning all about providing efficient services for our members and see this area of work as very similar to customer care in the commercial sector. It is important to be able to analyse and anticipate members' needs, communicate clearly with them and follow up all enquiries quickly and effectively.

I am now keen to start applying these skills in an organisation, where I can make a full contribution.

REFERENCES:

Mr J Phillips	Mr M Baldock (Director)
BTEC Graphic Design	Green World, Hunerk House
Course Director	99 North Street
North London Technical College	Bath
Swift Road	Avon
London NE178 3PU	BR4 2JK
Tel: 020 8830 0000	Tel: 01382 000000
e-mail: phillipsj@anyserve.co.uk	e-mail: baldock@gw.org.uk

Geraldine has only ever done voluntary work, but she uses the 'Additional Information' section to explain why. She had sensibly chosen voluntary work in the field in which she wanted to work, so is able to stress what useful experience she has gained.

Her years of volunteering have also gained her a glowing reference from the director of the charity concerned.

It is important for Geraldine that she makes as much of her voluntary experience as any other candidate would from paid work. She pulls out the main tasks that she contributed, evaluates the new areas that she has learnt about and describes those aspects that she particularly enjoyed. Employers are always interested in the motivation of applicants. It enables them to see if the things that inspired you in your previous work are linked to the work being offered. An enthusiastic candidate will shine even at the stage of submitting CVs or paper applications.

You can use your CV to confront any prejudices that employers may have about you. At first glance, Geraldine's work history is not very impressive. After studying arts subjects, she has not even had one 'proper' job. Employers may be tempted to assume that she is:

- lazy
- unable to hold down a job
- undisciplined
- not a team player
- stuck in a rut
- not interested in learning
- not ambitious.

In fact Geraldine is none of these things. She had to relinquish her career plans to look after her younger sister who was badly injured in a car crash. She explicitly confronts each of these possible perceptions by providing evidence of the contrary:

- Her hobbies show her active outlook.
- Her volunteering experience is evidence of her employability.

- Her six years of voluntary work show her rigour and discipline.
- She gives evidence of working as part of a team.
- She offers insight into best commercial practice and illustrates how she enjoys learning.
- She finishes by stating that she sees herself at the start of a new phase of career development.

The overall effect is that the employers would consider themselves lucky to get such a talented applicant – even though she has not had one paid job before. This, of course, is just the impression Geraldine was aiming at.

6. Many jobs

CURRICULUM VITAE

NAME: **Adam PETERS**

ADDRESS: 3 Upland Street
                     London SE21 1ST

TELEPHONE: 020 8946 0000

DATE OF BIRTH: 19 March 1975

NATIONALITY: British

EDUCATION:

Sept 1986– May 1991	Greens' School London SE3 1JK	**Subjects studied:** English, maths, science, art, metalwork, woodwork
Sept 1991– July 1992	Central College London SW1 3KA	**Which Job? Course**

EMPLOYMENT:

Aug 1999– Mar 2003	Freshfood Dairies London SW16	**Milk-roundsman:** Bookkeeping, dealing with the public, handling cash, ordering stock, banking and deliveries
Sept 1998– Apr 1999	True Personnel London E16 1HH	**Recruitment consultant:** Recruitment advertising, interviewing, wages, canvassing for new business, general office duties
July 1996– Aug 1998	Bales' Business Services London SE17 1JD	**Warehouseman:** Storing valuable data files, keeping accurate records, dealing with clients

Mar 1991– July 1996	Various temporary agencies around London, working as a general assistant and in manual work	
Aug 1989– Mar 1991	Jay's Stores London SE6 3RT	**Cashier:** Shelf-filling, responsible for cash, checking all deliveries, ordering shop stock

INTERESTS:

Squash, snooker, swimming, bowling, crosswords, collecting stamps, walking my dog.

ADDITIONAL INFORMATION:

I am always keen to take on extra responsibility at work. I am trustworthy and hard-working and have often worked overtime in my previous jobs.

My varied work experience has taught me a great deal about different types of organisations and I am confident at joining in quickly in any new position. I am a fast learner.

I would like to work in a position which involves contact with the public, as I get on well with a wide variety of people. I enjoy being part of a team, but can also work alone and unsupervised.

REFERENCES

Mr Hugh MacKinnon
(Foreman at Bales' Business Services)
14 Beach House
Brighton Road
London SE21 1HF

Tel: (work) 020 7493 0000

Mr Adrian Smithson
(Accountant)
134 Eugenia Road
London SW4 4TL

Tel: (work) 020 8699 0000

Adam has plenty of jobs listed on his CV already. He has grouped together some of his work experience, between 1991 and 1996, to cut further jobs out. Those that he is omitting only duplicate the jobs that he has listed in full elsewhere.

He gives full details of some jobs to show the skills that he has learned, grouping others together instead of listing them all.

Adam also has possible prejudices to overcome in the mind of potential employers. His rapid job changes over the years could worry anyone thinking of employing him in case it indicates a lack of persistence or determination. It could be the case that each of Adam's previous employers had been unhappy with his attitude or performance and that he had been encouraged to leave each job. Adam is keen to show that, although he may only have stayed for a short time in each place, he gave good value when he was there.

Many of us go through a period of trying out different types of work before we settle for one particular area. In fact the variety of practical work that Adam has been doing is quite consistent but just reflects the insecure nature of such work. More frequent job changing is becoming the norm in the modern world of work rather than the old pattern of spending years in one organisation. Promotion is normally gained now through moving to a different employer as hierarchies get flatter and prospects are limited accordingly.

In Adam's case, he is indeed someone who gets restless after too long in one place but he maintains his enthusiasm for work by moving on and starting with a new employer doing roughly similar work. This CV details all the different abilities that he has acquired over the years, which vary from clerical work to practical skills. He knows that demonstrating this will be vital if he is to get a job interview from his CV. His varied experience needs to show up as relatively more advantageous than his rapid moves are disadvantageous.

7. Gaps between jobs

CURRICULUM VITAE

NAME: **Shola ODUNTAN**

ADDRESS: 25b Aubert Road
                       Birmingham B15 1NS

TELEPHONE: 0121-661 0000

E-MAIL ADDRESS: s.oduntan@corfield.com

DATE OF BIRTH: 2 February 1975

NATIONALITY: Nigerian (with full British Citizenship)

MARITAL STATUS: Married

HEALTH: Excellent

EDUCATION:

| 1986–1991 | Government College Lagos, Nigeria | **O levels:** 5 subjects including English |
| 1991–1993 | Bournebrook College Birmingham B29 | **Course in Business Studies** |

EMPLOYMENT:

| 2000–2003 | Njoku Industries Birmingham B3 | **Marketing Assistant:** Responsible for all the marketing support activity for the company, producing and administering direct mail campaigns, creating and maintaining databases, planning, designing and implementing advertising, organising exhibitions, setting market budgets |

1996– 1998	Gold and Sons Birmingham B12	**Advertisement Production Manager:** Organising plans and advert layouts, liaising with clients and advertising agents, designers, printers, proof-reading and passing pages for filming and setting deadlines for the sections

ADDITIONAL INFORMATION:
In the mid 1990s I travelled extensively in Africa with a relative, supporting myself through trading activities. In 1999 I toured Europe, doing temporary, seasonal work. These periods of travelling have given me the opportunity to learn a great deal about other countries and cultures, and I have seen many different ways of organising businesses and society in general.

OTHER SKILLS:
During the last year, I have used a local resource centre to learn keyboarding and computer skills and am now able to use QuarkXpress, a desk-top publishing package. I can speak four different African languages and basic French.

INTERESTS:
Reading, listening to music, gardening, yoga and aerobics, writing short stories.

REFERENCES:
Mrs A Collins
Personnel Director
Njoku Industries
Wyndham Industrial Estate
Mill Lane
Birmingham B3 2DD
Tel: 0121-572 0000

Mr O Burkitt
Director, Gold and Sons
25 Field Lane
Birmingham B12 6LQ
Tel: 0121-283 0000

In order to explain the fact that she has had long gaps in her career history, Shola gives details about the periods that she spent travelling. She stresses the benefits that these periods have given her and shows how she has developed as a person.

She has only had two jobs so far and so she makes sure that she lists all the key tasks that she undertook in each place. If, like Shola, you know that there is one aspect of your CV that will need explaining, make sure you offer the details that are required. Any reader of this CV would wonder at the gaps between college and her first job, and between her two posts. Shola has ensured that she not only explains what she was doing during these periods but that she sells them as giving her advantages and skills not available to other candidates. The fact that she speaks four African languages could be invaluable to a company trading across that continent.

8. Woman returner

CURRICULUM VITAE

NAME:	**Barbara ANDERSON**
ADDRESS:	9 Redlands Tower Culvert Road Sidcup Kent DA15 3TT
TELEPHONE:	020 8300 0000
DATE OF BIRTH:	10 December 1975
NATIONALITY:	British

EDUCATION:

1986–1991	Sacred Heart Grammar School Sidcup Kent	**GCSEs:** 5 subjects including English
1991–1993	Sidcup Technical College Sidcup Kent	**A levels:** English C, History C

EMPLOYMENT:

Sept 1993–June 1997	Department of Employment Unemployment Benefit Office Mottingham Kent	**Executive Officer:** Supervising staff, organising work, dealing with the public, sorting out computer problems

OTHER SKILLS:

I am able to use computers and have recently learnt word-processing in my spare time.

INTERESTS:

I enjoy reading historical novels and biographies, going to the cinema and joining in outdoor activities with my children.

ADDITIONAL INFORMATION:

I was a prefect at school. In June 1997, I left the Civil Service to bring up my two young children. As a full-time mother since that date, I have acquired new skills, such as the ability to organise and communicate on different levels, to use my imagination, and to be patient and flexible.

REFERENCES:

Ms Irene Hill
22 Stafford Road
High Wycombe
Buckinghamshire
HW1 1LD

Tel: 01291 00000
e-mail: ihill@apex.com

Father Paul Behan
Parish Priest
Church of Our Lady
Crimscott Lane
London WC2B 1YB

Tel: 020 7832 0000

Barbara is anxious to get back to work after bringing up her young children. She sensibly stresses the skills that she has acquired during her time in the home and emphasises how keen she is to re-establish her career.

She gives full details of her previous job and shows that she has many interests.

Many women are apologetic if they have been out of the labour market for a while. Describing their activity as 'only bringing up my children', they downplay the skills that they have been developing during this period. In fact, raising children is hard work and demands many abilities that are not always obvious to other people. Other assets that might apply to someone in Barbara's position include:

- tolerance
- patience
- determination
- confidence
- using own initiative
- being a self-starter
- solving disputes
- good memory
- quick thinking
- setting boundaries and establishing discipline and routines
- problem solving
- project management
- administration
- managing finances
- being an effective entertainer!

If you have been bringing up children, make the most of the skills you have to offer as a result. Be proud of this real work in which you have been engaged and talk up what you have to offer an employer as a result.

9. Career changer

CURRICULUM VITAE

NAME:	**Marilyn BROWNE**
ADDRESS:	806 Tiverton Place London N5 2HX
TELEPHONE:	020 8928 0000
DATE OF BIRTH:	20 May 1970
MARITAL STATUS:	Divorced
NATIONALITY:	British
HEALTH:	Excellent

EDUCATION:

1983– 1988	Ragdale School Birmingham B14 1LJ	**O levels:** English A, Biology B, Maths B, History C, Chemistry B
1988– 1990	Charing Court Hospital London W5 2JN	**Pupil Nurse for State Enrolled Nurse**

EMPLOYMENT:

Nov 1997– Jan 2003	Queen's Hospital London SE3 2HJ	**State Enrolled Nurse:** Working in theatre with the Sister, making sure theatre list is correctly written, that theatre is ready for use, instruments are correct for different operations, teaching student nurses, completing appropriate paperwork, liaising between hospital departments, taking phone calls

June 1994– Aug 1997	Waterside Hospital London W1 3PP	**State Enrolled Nurse:** Looking after medical and surgical patients, doing ward rounds with doctors, making sure that patients' notes were up to date, transferring patients to theatre, dealing with enquiries, dispensing drugs
Nov 1990– May 1994	Charing Court Hospital London W5 2JN	**State Enrolled Nurse:** Working in out-patients' department, making sure patients' notes were completed, getting doctors' trays ready for examination, answering phone calls, dealing with patients and medical sales representatives

INTERESTS:
Horse-riding, badminton, walking my dog, learning keyboard skills, reading nursing journals.

ADDITIONAL INFORMATION:
My working life to date has been mainly caring for people. This has made me patient and tolerant when dealing with the public. In hospital, patients and their relatives are often scared and distressed, even angry, and they need calm but firm handling.

As a result of my State Enrolled Nurse training, I am familiar with the study of biology, chemistry and drugs, and have had 13 years' experience as a qualified nurse working in a variety of different medical establishments.

I now wish to use my professional skills in combination with my main interest, which is caring for animals. I feel my nursing skills together with my trustworthy, hard-working and dedicated character, would make me ideally suited to a career as an animal nurse.

REFERENCES:

Mr Simon Howarth (Theatre Manager) Queen's Hospital London SE3 2HJ Tel: 020 7339 0000	Mrs J Michaels 21 Green Vale London SE16 2KY Tel: 020 7231 0000

Marilyn wants to change her career after nearly 15 years studying and working in nursing. Although her experience will be very appropriate for her desired career in animal nursing, she needs to justify her decision to change her plans.

By using the 'Additional Information' section to explain her ideas, she can answer the questions which any future employer may have. This is important because an employer just flicking through a pile of CVs may not grasp that Marilyn wishes to change career direction unless she makes this fact stand out clearly in the document. Many people decide to take their skills and use them in a different way during their working lives. It may be that you find out about a new career after you have been working in one area for a while or you may just change your mind about what suits you best.

If you are in this position, it is up to you to establish your credentials for the new direction you wish to take. This will mean showing what transferable skills you have that will be applicable to your desired option. Marilyn spent some time establishing where the parallels lay between what she had been doing and what she wanted to change to. In her 'Additional Information' she includes three paragraphs that explain how her experience, skills and personality respectively are all suited to working as an animal nurse. This outline cannot help but impress the reader and encourage her candidature to be taken seriously as a result.

10. Made redundant

CURRICULUM VITAE

NAME:	**Melanie RANDALL**
ADDRESS:	5 Somerfield Street London SW9 4LH
TELEPHONE:	020 7889 0000
DATE OF BIRTH:	23 September 1976
NATIONALITY:	British
MARITAL STATUS:	Divorced

EDUCATION:

1987– 1992	Trinity School London SE8	**GCSEs:** English, Mathematics, Art, Geography, Domestic Science

EMPLOYMENT:

2000– 2002	Popular Pizzas London EC2	**Senior Assistant:** In charge of seven staff, organising work rotas, ordering stock, cashing-up, recruitment and training of staff, dealing with sales representatives
1997– 2000	Popular Pizzas London EC2	**Catering Assistant:** Helping to prepare fast food, general kitchen work, waiting at table and handling cash

---

| 1994– | Newgate Inn | **Kitchen Supervisor:** |
| 1996 | London E3 | In charge of busy kitchen, menu planning, cooking, cleaning, stock control, bookkeeping, banking and staff supervision |

| 1992– | Newgate Inn | **Kitchen Assistant:** |
| 1994 | London E3 | Helping out with serving, preparing food, and running special events |

INTERESTS:
Listening to music, reading, cooking and entertaining, and playing pool and darts. I arrange Charity Darts and Pool matches for the Multiple Sclerosis Society.

ADDITIONAL INFORMATION:
I am punctual, reliable and able to work enthusiastically under pressure, either within a team or alone. I am a straightforward, positive and a fair person with a friendly disposition and a good sense of humour. This has aided me in the supervision of staff and in extensive dealings with clients and the public.

I am always keen to contribute fully to every company I work for. I have been promoted in both my jobs and this reflected the high regard in which my skills were held.

I have been in positions of trust, handling money on behalf of others. I have a strong ethical outlook and am well-balanced and controlled. My aim is to find employment in an environment with high standards and productivity.

REFERENCES:

Dick Nye	Desmond Cook
Manager	Area Manager
The Newgate Inn	Popular Pizzas
Newgate Street	New Road
London E3 3FG	London EC2 3LR
Tel: 020 7447 0000	Tel: 020 7831 0000
e-mail: nye@newgate.com	e-mail: cookd@poppizza.com

Melanie had the misfortune to be made redundant, not once but twice, from her jobs in the catering trade. The first time it happened she had to start in a more lowly position and work her way back up again to a more responsible position – and now she has to begin again.

It is more difficult to find employment once you are unemployed, so she has filled the 'Additional Information' section with as much positive information about herself as possible. The 'Interests' section shows the charity fund-raising work that she is involved in, all of which adds to the impression that she has a lot to offer.

Melanie knows that a whole range of stereotypes can face someone who is out of work. She found out the first time she was made redundant that it was a slow process to get another job. Some of the assumptions that could be made about her are that she is:

- unemployable
- bound to be depressed
- unmotivated
- not able to keep to work routines or be disciplined
- bitter about her bad luck
- probably introverted
- someone with not much to offer
- an unreliable employee.

To combat these unfair and incorrect prejudices that she might face, she writes a positive and confident couple of paragraphs about her skills and personality in her 'Additional Information' section. The overall effect is upbeat and noticeable.

11. US style

CURRICULUM VITAE
FOR STEPHEN DEERY

PERSONAL PROFILE:
An analytical and proactive general manager with proven expertise in managing complex problems in multi-layered organisations. Has gained rapid promotion as a result of a determined approach and a progressive attitude to finding new solutions. A team player, comfortable with responsibility and keen to rise to opportunities, Stephen is available to join a lively team working in an organisation where he can contribute to the full.

ACHIEVEMENTS:
- Increased profits in present post by 50 per cent over five years.
- Spearheading new ways of working through Knowledge Management.
- Successfully completed demanding Management Trainee programme.
- Obtained promotion after impressing senior managers in my first post.
- Wide range of interests outside work that involve team collaboration.

RELEVANT EXPERIENCE:
- Team Leader, Ford Brothers – running Business Strategy team of seven, spearheading business decisions for the company. The business grew or shrank directly according to the decisions we took. The last five years have shown a steady increase in profits. Reporting directly to the Director of Sales and Strategy, recently developing new discipline of Knowledge Management for the company.

- Management Trainee, Appledore Analysis – achieved consistently high marks for endeavour and creative problem solving on this one-year programme. Specialised in using and developing new systems for improving project management across a wide range of applications. Promoted to Supervisor at the end of year.

EDUCATION:

1995	Charter College Godalming	BA Degree then a Diploma in Management Studies

INTERESTS:
A wide range of spare-time activities including windsailing in the summer, rugby in the winter, team running all year round and playing the piano with a musical group.

CONTACT:
Stephen Deery
14 Camberwell Road
Fentown
Warks CU3 9OP
Tel: 01200 000000
e-mail: Deery339045@freestate.co.uk

REFERENCES:
Tom Perks, Director of Sales and Strategy
Appledore Analysis
Fentown
Warks CU3 9LK

Tel 01200 100000
e-mail: perks@appan.co.uk

Joanne Stacey, Personnel Director
Ford Brothers
Wentforth
Warks CU14 2NN

Tel: 01289 000000
e-mail: joannes@Fordbro.com

Stephen's CV is written in the US style and it is a style that is becoming more common in the UK too. It starts with a definite and bold statement about his experience, achievements and qualities. This paragraph is aimed at 'selling' this jobseeker as someone worth taking note of. The advantage of this style is that the highlights are presented unapologetically right at the start of the document. It is saying: 'Look, this is what I have to offer – are you interested?' In more modern, international or sales-oriented businesses, the employers will be used to this kind of document. They will be happy to look at the first paragraph and decide whether or not to read more based on whether they like what they see there. No time is wasted if there is not a match between what the applicant is offering and the kind of person that the employer is looking for.

However, this also illustrates the disadvantages of this kind of CV. If it is presented to a more traditional, local or public sector organisation, the employer may be put off by the slightly more unusual 'take me or leave me' uncompromising tone. The hard sell will not be as successful here as the more gradual or gentle approach adopted in all the examples given previously. The format recommended there leads the reader in to the document by highlighting the writer's relevant education and experience. The format is more conservative but the advantage is that it will put fewer people off and could encourage more employers to dig deeper to find out more about the applicant.

12. Freestyle

CV HOLLY ENTWHISTLE

394 Central Parade
Longfield
N Yorkshire YO3 1XC

Tel: 01911 000 000
e-mail: holent@alop.com

PROFILE:
A self-motivated and creative manager, Holly has had 12 years' experience of leading teams in customer relations. She understands how to handle the range of customers' experience with products and services and her many achievements show the difference that she can make. Her calm attitude and skills with people ensure she offers a unique contribution to an organisation that is driven by its customers' opinions.

ACHIEVEMENTS:
- Increased customer satisfaction.
  In each role I have worked hard to increase customer satisfaction with the company. This sounds simple but involves giving detailed attention to a complex set of relationships and transactions, making sure that each one is as effective as possible.

- Reduced level of complaints.
  In my present job, the level of complaints now stands at a record low level. I devised a plan to reorganise the way that complaints from customers are handled and this has revolutionised the whole customer care strategy for the organisation.

- Greater team productivity.
  Customer relations go well if the team dealing with this area are motivated and efficient. I take a pride in the high ratings I have always received from my team in my regular 360-degree appraisal. My team rate me as firm but fair and know I am always open to hearing their point of view.

TRAINING:

I believe in lifelong learning. After a good general education and leaving college with a BTEC in Business Studies, I have continued my training through many short courses offered through the workplace. Over the last 10 years these include: advanced customer care, supervisory skills, motivating and leading effective teams, health and safety at work, personal image, and career development and planning.

OTHER SKILLS AND INTERESTS:

I do regular sponsored walks for a charity I support – and this activity keeps me fit. I sing in a local choir and we give public performances from time to time. This always makes me nervous but I enjoy it on the day. I try to go to the theatre and the cinema fairly frequently.

REFERENCES:

Rohini Truelove, Managing Director
Westcare Ltd
Stapley Business Centre
South Street
Hobbleton
Yorks YO9 IUU

Tel: 01773 000000
e-mail: rtruelove@westc.com

Cllr Kevin Didcot
Yately Health Authority
Southwold Civic Centre
Yately
Oxon OX3 3PL

Tel: 01998 000000
e-mail: didcot@yhah.org

In reality, many people produce a document that takes parts of the different styles and mixes them to produce a hybrid, or freestyle, CV that they feel most comfortable with. The example above illustrates this kind of layout.

Holly has written one of these freestyle CVs. She is mixing and matching layouts to produce a document that she feels will increase her chances of success. She uses the opening 'selling' paragraph that we saw in the last example, although the tone is slightly more gentle here. She has decided to lay out her work experience as a series of achievements relevant to the kind of job she is seeking, rather than just listing her chronological posts.

She summarises her education and training to highlight those areas that will be of particular interest to employers and shows her varied interests outside work. She has used a more unusual font to present her CV in the hope that this will add to its attractiveness.

6

Preparing your own CV

Step-by-step guide

Many points have been made in this book about the best way to prepare your own CV. It can seem daunting actually to get going when your head is full of all the possibilities. But it is important for your career that you make a start on preparing or updating your own document. The best time to do this is before there is an urgent need for you to have your CV ready – you need to devote enough time to its preparation to ensure that you do yourself justice. It is much more difficult to do this if you are in a big rush.

This section takes you step by step through the key points to recap on what has been suggested. Reading this chapter should help you to remember what has been said before and encourage you to focus on the key points for action. Getting started can be the hardest part of all, but, once you get going, you will find that the challenge of producing an impressive document seems easier straight away.

Step 1: Drafting your CV

Start the process of preparing your own CV by putting together a draft or rough version. Do this work at a time when you can put yourself into a positive frame of mind, and in a place where you can think creatively and work on presenting yourself in the best light. Choose a quiet time and place where you will not be disturbed, as you will need all of your concentration for the task. Using the blank form at the end of this chapter on pages 98–99, start to fill in all the sections, beginning with your personal details, through to your referees. Refer to Chapter 3 to help you to complete each section.

Education

In your first go at writing this document you should not hold back. At this stage you want to put in all the information that you can remember. Starting from your secondary education (age 11 onwards), include every school and college attended, each course studied and all qualifications gained. You can sift and evaluate this information later on, but it is easier to decide to leave material out than to find out that you do not have enough to include. Take yourself back to those days and try to think back to the time you spent at each of these places. Include any particular achievements or events that you remember.

Employment

Move on now to note down every employer that you have ever worked for, whether it was full- or part-time, holiday or voluntary work. This represents the essential raw material from which will come the finished version of your CV. You will not want to include every possible detail in the real thing but writing them down in rough will help you to decide what to use later on. Try to be as accurate as possible with the relevant dates.

Other skills

Rack your brains for things to add to this section. Driving licence, first aid, computer and word-processing skills would all fit in here. There may be some particular skills that are relevant to the job you are applying for that you have not been able to include elsewhere, such as using certain tools, machinery or equipment. Language ability should be mentioned in this part of the document. There may be specific practical training courses that you have attended that fit into this section, eg computer courses, customer care, sales and marketing or management.

Interests

For this draft CV, include any pastimes or hobbies that you have ever spent time on, to give you a list from which to choose three or four sporty pursuits; then write down the same number of activities which show your other interests. The more you can show that you are an 'all-rounder', the better. Include interests that show you can use your brain as well as your hands and those that illustrate that you enjoy team involvement as well as solo work.

Additional information

This is the section where you can really go to town. If you want your CV to jump out at an employer, use this space to pick out your particular strengths. Just write down what your best friend, or perhaps your mother, would say about you – on a good day! How would they describe your best points to an employer?

Don't worry about sounding boastful. This is the only information that employers will have to go on, so this section is telling them that they should definitely invite you for an interview. Remember only to talk about what you have to offer. Illustrate what you think you can contribute in the right position. Create two paragraphs as a minimum here.

References

Include two referees who will help create a good impression about you. Check with both your referees that they are quite happy to be included in your CV. Make sure that their details are correct and include full and current contact details including their e-mail addresses.

Step 2: Editing your CV

Now read everything you have written down so far and decide what to include or delete. You will need to spend the most time on the 'Education' and 'Employment' sections. The rule here is – if in doubt, leave it out, so the only information that remains is clear, concise and interesting to read. It must tell the story of your career to date, stressing your achievements and showing your development.

Look through the examples in Chapter 5 to see the sort of information that other people have included in their CVs. Look at each section of your draft document and try to think what needs to be included to give a fair picture of your experience. This step can only be done by you, but remember that the whole CV should only cover two sheets of A4 paper; you will not have room for anything but the essential information. Ask yourself 'Does this part of the CV add to the total impression?' before you leave it in. Be alert to the need to update regularly the terms you use. 'Word processors' are now just referred to as 'computers'. The 'World Wide Web' is now usually referred to as the 'Internet'. Words change over time and you do not want to appear to be out of touch. Check also the kind of words you are using. Moderate words will appear mediocre, so exchange them for bolder, bigger language, eg 'achieved', 'successful', 'maximised', 'enjoy', 'relish', 'satisfaction'.

At this stage, enlist a friend or relative to take an objective look at what you have written. They may be able to tell you if some information needs to made clearer, or if some parts of the CV are too long or too short. They may also be able to spot mistakes that you have completely ignored. Leave the document for a couple of days, and then return to it to evaluate again if it is creating the impression you are looking for. Consider if you want to vary the layout or if you are happy that the traditional format is the best one for your purposes. See Chapter 5 for alternatives.

Step 3: The final version

Now check through everything you have written. If you are sure it is all correct and accurate, then you are ready to get the final version typed up.

However good the person is who types up your CV, you must make sure that you check and re-check the document for accuracy of content and attractive presentation. If your CV is produced on a word processor, it will be a fairly simple matter to make corrections; time spent proof-reading at this stage will save having to hurry later on.

Once the document has been typed up, show it to somebody else. Another person will often be able to spot errors that you will miss, however many times you reread it.

If you now feel happy that your CV is a good representation of your strengths and assets, the real test is to use it to apply for jobs and to contact employers.

Step 4: The covering letter

You will never send out your CV on its own. At the very least, you will write a letter to the employer saying which job you are applying for. Even if a covering letter has not specifically been requested, you can use the opportunity to explain more about yourself.

What goes in a covering letter?

In most cases you will need to say why you are sending your CV, a little about yourself and what you want to happen next. A letter one to two pages in length can reiterate what you have to offer an employer. Go back to the list of your best qualities that you used for the 'Additional Information' section and restate the key points in a different form in the letter.

Obviously, all letters will be personal to the writer, but here are some general hints about the way to put your covering letter together, followed by an example:

● Keep the letter reasonably brief – the employer has already got two pages of your CV to read. The letter should never be longer than two sides of A4 paper.

- This is your introduction to your CV – make sure your letter is interesting enough for your CV to be actually read. Think of this letter as a sales document. Use short sentences and positive words to create a memorable and attractive impression.
- Always be very courteous – it costs you nothing and politeness cannot help but impress the reader.
- Use new, unlined paper to create a good impression. The covering letter can be word-processed or typed. Handwriting is much more unusual these days. If it must be handwritten ensure it is *extremely* neat. Use the same type of paper as you did for the CV if possible, so they match.
- Take as much care over the letter as you have with your CV. Your hard work on the CV may be wasted if the employer takes a dislike to a hasty or messy letter, and throws the lot into the waste-paper bin.
- If you are sending your CV in response to an advertisement, make sure that you address the letter to the correct person, and say where you saw the vacancy. The company may be advertising several jobs at the same time, in different publications, and will need to know which one you are applying for.
- If this is a speculative letter, it always stands more chance of success if it is addressed to someone in particular. So if you are approaching employers who may have vacancies, but who have not yet advertised, try to find out the name of the person you want to approach and address the letter to him or her personally.
- Shrug off the worry that your letter sounds boastful. It needs to be larger than life to get you noticed.
- Attach the letter to your CV with a paperclip so it does not get separated.

Example of a covering letter

Dear Ms Charnley

I enclose my curriculum vitae for your attention. I am a 31 year-old mother of two children. As you can see from my CV, I have five years' experience of clerical work in a busy office and have recently completed a word-processing course at a local training centre.

I thoroughly enjoy working in administration and I know that unless the paperwork is accurate any company will suffer. Therefore I am careful about checking my work and always help my colleagues out to get the work done.

I am highly motivated, ambitious and enjoy working to deadlines. I have excellent references and would relish the chance to work as part of the team at White Brothers.

I should be grateful if you would contact me if you have any vacancies in your company, or keep my information on file in case of future openings.

Thank you for your attention in this matter. I look forward to hearing from you.

Yours sincerely

Helen Guyer

Step 5

Now carefully save a copy of your CV and covering letter, both on computer and on paper, if possible. This forms a vital record of those employers you approach, or positions you apply for.

If you send out your CV and do not get a reply, it is always worth ringing the company in three or four weeks' time, to check if there is any news. Following up politely in this way can help you eliminate those employers who are definitely not interested.

Conclusion

Your CV is a tool for job-seeking purposes. Like any other tool, its value lies in the manner in which you use it. Keep abreast of the way the world of work is changing. Be interested in articles about what employers are looking for. Use your CV if you are looking for work. Make sure friends in the same line of work have a copy. Get opinions from others about how effective a document they believe it to be. Look at other people's documents to see how they have compiled theirs.

Think of this CV of yours as a living, breathing organism that requires feeding to keep it operating at peak efficiency. If you are in work, your CV needs updating with every new job, promotion or change in your responsibilities. If you start new interests or experience achievements in work, education or voluntary work, add these. If you develop your personality in a new direction or get different positive feedback from a manager about yourself, enhance the 'Additional Information' section straight away. If you change your mind about your career direction, draft another version of your CV in case you find an opportunity to develop in this area.

Points to remember

- Work hard to produce a document of which you feel proud.
- The best time to do work on your CV is when you do not need it urgently.
- A meek outline of your strengths is not enough, so boast!
- Use different versions of your CV if you feel different career directions warrant it.

Dos and don'ts

Dos

DO   experiment with different fonts, layouts and contents of your CV, but remember to keep it simple, straightforward and clear, whichever you choose.

DO   reject any information that does not enhance your impact with employers, and keep evaluating your CV to ensure it stays the best it can be.

DO   take as much care with a covering letter so that your CV gets the chance to do its work on your behalf.

Don'ts

DON'T   leave your CV to moulder in a drawer and be caught unawares with a document that needs a lot of work.

DON'T   take rejection personally; there may just have been a more suitable person for the position this time.

DON'T   give up if you are knocked back – the right job could be just around the next corner.

Good luck!

Blank CV

CURRICULUM VITAE

NAME:

ADDRESS:

TELEPHONE NUMBER:

DATE OF BIRTH:

NATIONALITY:

MARITAL STATUS:

EDUCATION:

(Dates)   (Name and location)   (Qualifications or subjects
                                      studied)

EMPLOYMENT:

(Dates)   (Name and location)   (Position held and main
                                      duties)

OTHER SKILLS:

INTERESTS:

ADDITIONAL INFORMATION:

REFERENCES:

7

Using the Internet

Using the Internet to help you prepare your CV

There are many sites on the Internet that give you assistance with compiling a CV. Most are sites displaying job vacancies. They make their money from recruitment advertising from employers or by taking a commission from companies if they place you in a job. As part of the information they provide around searching for jobs, these sites often include tips on CVs, interview skills and other career development issues. Jobseekers can access these pages free of charge, although, if you want to use their specialised targeting process for locating the most relevant jobs to suit you, you may be required to go through a registration process.

Many sites exist either to help you compile a full CV (companies usually charge for this service) or to distribute a shorter free version on your behalf to targeted companies. Known as an 'online CV', this is a CV produced to a formula layout that can be quickly completed and distributed on your behalf. Essentially, completing an online CV is a matter of filling in the boxes on the screen in front of you to create lists of your experience, qualifications and abilities. These CVs are therefore not personally designed documents.

Free services could well be worth sampling in case they bring up new contacts. Be careful though about paying money online for a service of this kind, unless you are sure that the benefits will be worth it. Try to talk to people who have used the service before you spend money on it. A scrappy formulaic CV sent as junk mail along with many others to unwilling recipients may not enhance your chances of success.

Applying for jobs online

Many organisations now recruit directly through the Internet. They assess application forms and CVs that have been sent in to their organisation or they search specialised recruitment sites to find applicants who might be suitable for their vacancies. It is both cheaper and quicker for companies to accept online applications. They do not have to pay a recruitment agency and they (and you) can access the applications any time of the day.

Do not be scared of using the Internet as a method of posting your CV to employers. It can be a powerful way of getting yourself in front of employers and shows you can handle new technology. For some jobs it is now the main way to apply – in the IT sector, for example.

Electronic application and selection methods mean that your document may appear different at its destination from the way it looked when you e-mailed it. It may also change again when dealt with, copied or scanned at the employer's premises. This means that applications for this kind of delivery need to be constructed and presented in a way that takes account of how they will be sent, received and processed.

Using keywords

When recruiters search through CVs electronically they will do so by looking for keywords in each document. So what are keywords? Recruiters identify certain trigger words that they feel should be covered by candidates who stand a chance of being successful for their vacancy. Keywords tend to be nouns describing the kind of work applicants have done in the past that will be directly relevant to the job on offer, eg:

- management
- administration
- organisation
- supervision.

Or else they refer to the name of the position held, eg:

- manager
- administrator
- supervisor.

Or they refer to the name of the specific skill or knowledge required, eg:

- Word
- Excel
- PowerPoint.

You can see how these keywords are similar to the transferable skills required by an employer, just specified by single words that identify the key skills and attributes concerned.

Employers searching by keywords will select any CV for further consideration that mentions a critical number of the keywords identified. Furthermore they may want certain words to be given a high priority by the successful candidates. If you leave the fact that you have managed teams to the last paragraph in your CV, you may not get selected to be interviewed for a relevant position where managing staff is a priority task.

Identifying the keywords that may be used for a job that interests you will mean that you have to do some thinking and researching about the job. If it is a type of employment that you are already familiar with, think about the many topical words that get used often and try to incorporate the most familiar into this version of your CV. If it is a new work area that you are trying to break into, research through professional journals, talking to people in the business and closely examining adverts for similar positions to discover the keywords that frequently occur.

Scannable CVs

Some employers accept paper CVs and then scan them into a recruitment software package. This reads the CV and prioritises it by matching it by keywords. Scanners cannot always read bold or italic print, so a plain layout for your CV is recommended if you know it is likely to be scanned on receipt. Any CV that is longer than one page is unlikely to be dealt with so keep your CV brief if you know it is likely to be scanned – leave out the less relevant parts of your full version, such as interests.

Electronic CVs

In order for your CV to be instantly readable by any package that may receive it, you need to write and save it in the lowest common denominator of formats. Plain text format is the most common Internet format. You will need to use *, + or – instead of bullet points, just as you do in e-mails.

- Set the margins at 6.5 inches.
- Write in Courier 12 point so that you get 65 characters per line of text.
- Write with no bold, underlining or italics so that your document can be interpreted in any package.
- Do not use fancy graphics as this may not be clear on receipt.
- Save as a 'text only' document when prompted how you wish to save it.
- Check it in a text editor such as Notepad in Windows to check how it will look to an employer on receipt.

- Add at the end that you can also provide the document in whatever format you normally use, eg Word.

E-mailing your CV

The e-mail that you attach to your CV should include the same content as a covering letter for a CV that you post. Attach the CV both in Word and as a text file for ease of viewing.

Filling in an online application form or e-form

This is an electronic version of an application form that requires you to input text into specific boxes, or fields, and then send this information to the employer's or recruiter's Web site. If the questions tally, you can copy and paste information direct from the text version of your CV.

CV banks

Some Web sites exist just to hold online CVs in a data bank, which can then be accessed by employers looking for candidates. You may have to pay for this service but you may find that it is an effective way of finding out about new vacancies if you have impressive previous experience and transferable skills. You will often be asked to input a geographical area within which you would be interested in working.

Useful sites

Some sites specialise in recruitment, others feature a recruitment page and company or organisation sites may also show vacancies within that organisation. Some sites work as online recruitment agencies, allowing you to lodge your details with them in the form of your CV. Employers know they can search through the CVs held online to look for suitable candidates.

Security

Think carefully about where and how you post your CV online. If it is an open site with easy access by employers, you may find that your current boss sees that you are searching around for a new job. Would this be a problem for you?

Points to remember

- Many more employers are using online recruitment to save themselves time and money. It is now the standard way to recruit for jobs in some sectors.
- It is more work to prepare your CV to be accessed online but it could increase your chances of being picked out by an employer.
- Only attempt to send an online CV if you have ensured that it will be an impressive document once received by the employer.
- You still need to find out all you can about the organisation to help you present the most impressive application you can and to make your CV stand out from the crowd.

Dos and don'ts

Dos

DO   update your CV regularly so that, if employers only want to see the most recent, yours will be near the top of the pile.

DO   always include full contact details and your e-mail address.

DO   spend time getting the correct keywords in your CV. Examine carefully all the information you can about the employer and the vacancy concerned. Look too at other details for similar jobs at the right level. Use all the significant nouns that describe the key activities in the job or the characteristics required.

Don'ts

DON'T apply for more than one job in one company. It will look as though you are applying indiscriminately because you are desperate.

DON'T   just sit back and wait after you have applied online. You still need to be conducting other job search activities in case you have no success from this approach.

DON'T   think because you are applying online that presentation is less important. It is just as important but different methods need to be used to make sure you create the best impression.

The 10 best sites for jobseekers

The Internet is a fast-changing scene and new sites appear as fast as others fall from view. Here are 10 of the current best for UK jobseekers:

1.   www.timesonline.co.uk
     The Web site of the *Times* newspaper group, which contains Appointments – their jobs pages. It is particularly useful for senior vacancies and managerial, technical and senior secretarial positions. This site includes CV pointers, topical interview tips and career development articles.

2.   www.prospects.ac.uk
     Labelled as the UK's official graduate careers Web site, this site is provided by the Higher Education Careers Services Unit and the Association of Graduate Careers Advisory Services. It is aimed at graduates and provides 'the essential guide to graduate careers and postgraduate study in the UK' according to the home page. Accessible and functional, this is a useful resource for graduates and, by gathering all the key points together, can help to focus graduate job search or paths to further study. Articles give pointers to compiling a CV and there is extensive job search information and advice here.

3.   www.jobs.guardian.co.uk
     'The UK's most popular newspaper website', provided by the *Guardian* newspaper group, which owns the national

newspaper with the largest selection of jobs. This site is accessible and impressive, and is easy to search for jobs by relevance to your needs. It has many new jobs every day, listed by broad sector and seniority so is worth checking on a regular basis for national-level jobs. You can complete a profile on this site to which your CV can be attached. This electronic document can then be made available to specific employers who may be interested in you. There is no charge for this service. You can also send your CV to any vacancy that interests you.

4.   www.ft.com
      This is the recruitment site provided by the *Financial Times* newspaper. It includes job vacancies, particularly in the financial sector and has some job search tips.

5.   www.jobs.co.uk
      Labelling itself 'The one-stop jobs supersite', this helpful site searches all of the UK jobs boards for you to find vacancies that may suit you. It offers a list of sites that can help with CVs and assesses them for amount of information, ease of use, etc. This site includes interview and applications advice and links up direct to all the sites it finds for you.

6.   www.doctorjob.com
      Doctorjob is a careers publisher's Web site featuring a lot of careers information and graduate employment opportunities displayed in a quirky style with cartoons.

7.   www.reed.co.uk
      This site is owned by Reed employment, a leading employment agency. It includes voluntary opportunities and career tips including CV advice and interview techniques.

8.   www.bradleycvs.co.uk
      This Web site is produced by a company that offers a CV writing service for a fee. The site is useful, offering free information on compiling a CV and examples of CVs. It also has articles on job search skills including interview

techniques. This site has many links to other specific recruitment sites across the Internet.

9. www.monster.co.uk
   A commercial recruitment Web site with extensive job search advice included.

10. www.jobpilot.co.uk
    A recruitment Web site with some CV tips included.

Other useful sites

General vacancy sites

www.jobs-at.co.uk
www.jobs1.co.uk
www.jobtrack.co.uk
www.justpeople.com
www.peoplebank.co.uk
www.stepstone.co.uk
www.topjobs.co.uk
www.ukjobs.com

Public sector jobs Web site

www.jobsgopublic.co.uk

CV writing and posting

www.cvspecial.co.uk

Company Web sites

Employment Service: www.employmentservice.gov.uk
Royal British Legion (ex-servicemen and women): www.rbli.co.uk
General business directory: www.ukbusinesspark.co.uk
Confederation of British Industry: www.cbi.org.uk

Listing of recruitment agencies: www.ipl.co.uk/recruit.html

Newspaper and publishers' sites

TES: www.jobs.tes.co.uk
Telegraph: www.appointments-plus.com
Evening Standard (London vacancies): www.standard.co.uk
Summary of local newspapers' jobs: www.fish4jobs.co.uk

Other sources of help

The Connexions Service

In some areas of the country, the staff in your local Connexions Service can offer help and advice to adults. They will have reference books about employers and applying for jobs, and understanding, skilled staff who can help you put your CV together if you get stuck. Find the telephone number in the local phone book and ring them to speak to a careers or personal adviser to find out more.

Employment Agencies

Agencies may wish to compile a CV for you for a particular type of job to help them to 'sell' you to an employer. They charge the employer if you are placed with a company and you will not always be allowed to have a copy of the CV they compile for your own use.

Private Careers Counsellors

You can get help from careers counsellors who work privately and who make a charge for their service. This can be very expensive and although they will help you to put the CV together and then print it out on a top quality printer, you will also be charged extra for any reprints and amendments that you may require in the future.

Learn Direct Helpline

The Learn Direct number, 0800 100 900, is a Government funded telephone helpline available to everyone. Ring the freephone number and you will be given advice about local sources of help on careers and learning issues. This could include where to contact the types of organisations mentioned above.

Further reading from Kogan Page

Career, Aptitude and Selection Tests, Jim Barrett, 1998

How to Master Personality Questionnaires, 2nd edn, Mark Parkinson, 2000

How to Master Psychometric Tests, 2nd edn, Mark Parkinson, 2000

How to Pass Advanced Aptitude Tests, Jim Barrett, 2002

How to Pass Advanced Numeracy Tests, Mike Bryon, 2002

How to Pass Computer Selection Tests, Sanjay Modha, 1994

How to Pass Graduate Psychometric Tests, 2nd edn, Mike Bryon, 2001

How to Pass Numeracy Tests, 2nd edn, Harry Tolley and Ken Thomas, 2000

How to Pass Numerical Reasoning Tests, Heidi Smith, 2003

How to Pass Professional-level Psychometric Tests, Sam Al-Jajjoka, 2001

How to Pass Selection Tests, 2nd edn, Mike Bryon and Sanjay Modha, 1998

How to Pass Technical Selection Tests, Mike Bryon and Sanjay Modha, 1993

How to Pass the Civil Service Qualifying Tests, 2nd edn, Mike Bryon, 2003

How to Pass the Police Initial Recruitment Test, Harry Tolley, Ken Thomas and Catherine Tolley, 1997

How to Pass Verbal Reasoning Tests, 2nd edn, Harry Tolley and Ken Thomas, 2000

How to Succeed at an Assessment Centre, Harry Tolley and Bob Wood, 2001

Rate Yourself!, Marthe Sansregret and Dyane Adams, 1998

Test Your Creative Thinking, Lloyd King, 2003

Test Your Emotional Intelligence, Bob Wood and Harry Tolley, 2002

Test Your IQ, Ken Russell and Philip Carter, 2000

Test Your Own Aptitude, 3rd edn, Jim Barrett and Geoff Williams, 2003

Test Yourself!, Jim Barrett, 2000

The Times Book of IQ Tests – Book Three, Ken Russell and Philip Carter, 2003

The Times Book of IQ Tests – Book Two, Ken Russell and Philip Carter, 2002

The Times Book of IQ Tests – Book One, Ken Russell and Philip Carter, 2001

Also available on CD ROM in association with *The Times*

Published by Kogan Page Interactive, *The Times* Testing Series is an exciting new range of interactive CD ROMs that will provide invaluable, practice tests for both job applicants and for those seeking a brain-stretching challenge. Each CD ROM features:

- over 1000 unique interactive questions;
- instant scoring with feedback and analysis;
- hours of practice with randomly generated tests;
- questions devised by top UK MENSA puzzles editors and test experts;
- against-the-clock, real test conditions.

Current titles available:

Brain Teasers Volume 1, 2002
Psychometric Tests Volume 1, 2002
Test Your IQ Volume 1, 2002
Test Your Aptitude Volume 1, 2002

Interview and career guidance

The A–Z of Careers and Jobs, 10th edn, Irene Krechowiecka, 2002
Act Your Way Into a New Job, Deb Gottesman and Buzz Mauro, 1999
Changing Your Career, Sally Longson, 2000
Choosing Your Career, Simon Kent, 1997
Creating Your Career, Simon Kent, 1997
From CV to Shortlist, Tony Vickers, 1997
Graduate Job Hunting Guide, Mark Parkinson, 2001
Great Answers to Tough Interview Questions, 5th edn, Martin John Yate, 2001
How You Can Get That Job!, 3rd edn, Rebecca Corfield, 2002
The Job-Hunters Handbook, 2nd edn, David Greenwood, 1999
Job-Hunting Made Easy, 3rd edn, John Bramham and David Cox, 1995
Landing Your First Job, Andrea Shavick, 1999
Net That Job!, 2nd edn, Irene Krechowiecka, 2000
Odd Jobs, 2nd edn, Simon Kent, 2002
Offbeat Careers, 3rd edn, Vivien Donald, 1995
Online Job-Hunting: Great Answers to Tough Interview Questions, Martin John Yate and Terra Dourlain, 2001
Readymade CVs, 2nd edn, Lynn Williams, 2000
Readymade Job Search Letters, 2nd edn, Lynn Williams, 2000
Successful Interview Skills, 3rd edn, Rebecca Corfield, 2002
Your Job Search Made Easy, 3rd edn, Mark Parkinson, 2002

Kogan Page Careers Series

These practical guides range from *Careers in Accountancy* to *Careers in the Theatre*. They are packed with useful information. School and college leavers, graduates and anyone considering a career change will find the books an invaluable source of information and help in planning their future careers. All titles contain details of:

- careers openings and prospects
- educational requirements and training opportunities
- how to apply for jobs
- likely working conditions
- university and college courses.

The above titles are available from all good bookshops. For further information, please contact the publisher at the following address:

Kogan Page Limited
120 Pentonville Road
London N1 9JN
Tel: 020 7278 0433
Fax: 020 7837 6348
www.kogan-page.co.uk

Index

£7.99